gud

ltd to 750

HARVARD KEATS MEMORIAL STUDIES

NUMBER I

LONDON : GEOFFREY CUMBERLEGE

OXFORD UNIVERSITY PRESS

KEATS' REPUTATION
IN AMERICA
TO 1848

By

HYDER EDWARD ROLLINS

1946

CAMBRIDGE, MASSACHUSETTS

HARVARD UNIVERSITY PRESS

DESIGNED BY BURTON J. JONES, JR.

ILLUSTRATIONS

KEATS' REPUTATION IN AMERICA
TO 1848

THE DECLINE, fall, and rise of Keats' reputation in Great Britain has been discussed by various writers, as T. R. Lounsbury,[1] Sir Sidney Colvin,[2] Messrs. G. L. Marsh and N. I. White,[3] and Mr. G. H. Ford.[4] Colvin, in sketching the poet's "after-fame," concluded that "soon after the mid-century . . . the battle for his fame, at least among the younger generations, [was] won. He has counted for the last sixty years and more, alike in England and in America, as an uncontested great poet, whose works, collected or singly, have been in demand in edition after edition."[5] But these words give an inaccurate outline of the situation in America, where long before the mid-century Keats was widely talked about and written about as a great poet. Nothing short of a sizable volume could record the American vogue, much less the influence, of Keats to date. Meanwhile, it may be of some interest to sketch more or less chronologically, if incompletely, the growth of his reputation up to the appearance of Milnes' biography in 1848, indicating when and how he first became known in America, what editions of his verse were published, and who were his earliest disciples, editors, and critics.

THE PUBLISHER John Taylor often commented on the slowness with which Keats' poems sold in England,[1] and it is extremely doubtful that many copies of the 1817, 1818, and 1820 volumes made their way to America, although magazines (like the New York *Literary and Scientific Repository*, October, 1820[2]), following London journals, sometimes announced their publication. Hence it was scarcely to be expected that the compiler of *Elegant Extracts of Poetry* (Hartford, Connecticut, 1818) should have been able to include selections from them; and while he professes to represent "each of the celebrated living bards in Great-Britain," his romantic poets are limited to Campbell, Byron, Moore, Southey, Wordsworth, Hunt, and Scott. Copies of the 1817 and 1818 poems were sent by Keats to his brother George[3] in Louisville, Kentucky; but as late as April 10, 1824, George wrote to C. W. Dilke that he had "not even the last book that he [John] published," and asked "if it sustained or injured his poetical reputation."[4]

Mr. T. O. Mabbott[5] believes that the obscure young author, Elizabeth Denning, of *Poems* (New York, 1821) had seen the 1820 volume, and that by taking an adjective from "The Grecian Urn" "she has a strong claim to be the earliest poet to show the influence of Keats in America."[6] Perhaps on the basis of his *Literary Remains* (Hartford, 1832), edited by J. G. Whittier,[7] a stronger claim could be made for Keatsian (as well as Byronic) influence on John G. C. Brainard (who died in 1828). A reader of "To an Antique Female Bust"[8] is reminded at once—by idea, not language—of "The Grecian Urn."

> . . . Time who does not spare
> The most divine of human forms, has left
> On thy pale brow no wrinkle,—nor bereft
> Thee of a single charm;—ages have swept
> O'er thy fair head, but still thy cheek has kept
> Its sheen and smoothness. . . .
> Death has no claims
> On thee thou fair one! thou'lt exist when we,
> Who now behold thy charms shall mould'ring be
> In earth; and others will arise, and gaze,
> And bow before thee,—still will beauty's rays
> Beam from thee, bright, as though thou just had'st sprung,
> New into life—still beautiful, still young!

But this particular imitation of Keats is not in the *Occasional Pieces of Poetry* (New York, 1825) Brainard himself had published three years before his death; and by the publishers of the Hartford, 1841 (misdated 1842), edition of his *Poems* it is omitted as one of several poems in Whittier's volume which "were not the productions of the muse of Brainard," but "are from

3

the pens of gentlemen better known in other walks than those of poesy."

A poet far more distinguished than Miss Denning or Brainard, Joseph Rodman Drake (to the disgust of Sir Edmund Gosse he was often referred to as "the American Keats"), appears to have been Keats' first real disciple.[9] On a visit to London in the spring of 1818 he bought a copy of *Endymion,* which became his "favorite volume," and, back in New York, he "used to read aloud" from it to his drug-store partner, Dr. William Langstaff, and to his poet-friend, Fitz-Greene Halleck. After his untimely death in September, 1820, it was among Halleck's "most prized possessions."[10] Halleck himself, bearing letters of introduction to Byron, Campbell, Moore, Scott, Southey, and Wordsworth, reached Liverpool on July 21, 1822. In London he haunted the bookshops, at one of which he met Hobhouse and saw Coleridge.[11] Presumably he talked about Keats with his English friends, but his own verse seems mainly to be influenced by Scott, Campbell, and Byron.

Occasionally other visitors in England learned something of Keats. The painter Washington Allston, an intimate friend of Haydon, Severn, Southey, Wordsworth, and Coleridge, during his second sojourn there (1811–1818) came to admire the poet's work. Severn, especially, was "struck with the clear and independent manner in which Washington Allston, in the year 1818, expressed his opinion of John Keats's verse, when the young poet's writings first appeared, amid the ridicule

4

of most English readers." Severn, who knew nothing of Drake or Halleck, continued: "Mr. Allston was at that time the only discriminating judge among the strangers to Keats who were residing abroad," and he said of the early poems, "They are crude materials of real poetry, and Keats is sure to become a great poet."[12]

Before 1829 most Americans derived what information they had about Keats from the brutal reviews of the *Quarterly* and *Blackwood's* or from the eulogies in the periodicals of Hunt and others. Such magazines were imported in large numbers, many were reproduced in American editions, while eclectic journals made up entirely of reprints from British periodicals were not uncommon. George Keats told Dilke on April 20, 1825, that he read "several works published in America that regularly extract the most interesting articles from the English periodicals." As a result, careful American readers learned about as much of Keats' life and work as the average English reader of the day.

As an illustration, the Boston *Atheneum; Or, Spirit of the English Magazines*, October 15, 1817,[13] took from the *European Magazine*, May, 1817,[14] an article on "Keats' Poems" which, on the whole, flatters the poet, saying that "for the grand, elaborate, and abstracted music of nature our author has a fine ear," and that his volume "is full of imaginations and descriptions . . . delicate and elegant." More favorable still was the review, this time of the *Lamia* volume, which on November 1, 1820,[15] the *Atheneum* reprinted from the *New*

Monthly Magazine.[16] After commenting on these "pieces of calm beauty, or of lone and self-supported grandeur," it goes on to express "wonder at the gigantic stride which he [Keats] has taken." Then the Philadelphia *Saturday Magazine,* October 20, 1821,[17] reproduced from the London *Literary Gazette*[18] a brief note: "P. Bysche [*sic*] Shelley has a piece in the press in honour of the deceased poet Keats, whose death is therein ascribed to the inhumanity of his reviewers!" In subsequent issues, November 3 and 17, 1821,[19] it reprinted from the *London Magazine*[20] a long review of Keats' 1820 volume, which gives a favorable judgment on the poems and one most unfavorable to the abuse of Christopher North and J. W. Croker.

Lady Morgan, after the publication of *Italy* (1821), was attacked by the English reviews as savagely as Keats had ever been. Her book was popular in America, and when she replied in self-defense (September 15, 1821) Americans could readily have seen the original "Letter to the Reviewers of 'Italy' " in the *New Monthly Magazine*[21] or else the reprints in the Philadelphia *Literary Gazette: Or, Journal of Criticism*[22] or the New York *Literary and Scientific Repository.*[23] Probably many of them noticed her two references to a writer named "Keates," especially the first in which she asserts that the *Quarterly* reviewers "sent the sensitive, the ingenious Keates, to an early grave!"

Fuller information about the victim was provided by the Boston *Atheneum,* which on March 1, 1822,[24] reproduced from John Millard's annual, *Time's Telescope*, January, 1822,[25] an article, "Death of John Keats, the Poet," itself largely borrowed from the *London Magazine*.[26]

> Some, in their age,
> Ripe for the sickle; others, *young, like him,*
> And falling green beneath th'untimely stroke.

MR. KEATS died at Rome, Feb. 23, 1821, whither he had gone for the benefit of his health. His complaint was a *consumption*, under which he had languished for some time; but his death was accelerated by a cold caught in his voyage to Italy. It is rather singular, that, in the year 1816, he expressed an ardent desire to visit the shores of Italy, in one of his earliest productions, and is too beautiful to be omitted in this humble tribute to his memory. [The sonnet, "Happy is England," is quoted.]

Mr. Keats was, in the truest sense of the word, a POET. There is but a small portion of the public acquainted with the writings of this young man: yet they were full of high imagination and delicate fancy, and his images were beautiful and more entirely his own, perhaps, than those of any living writer whatever. He had a fine ear, a tender heart, and at times great force and originality of expression; and notwithstanding all this, he has been suffered to rise and pass away almost without a notice: the laurel has been awarded (for the present) to other brows; the bolder aspirants have been allowed to take their station on the slippery steps of the Temple of Fame, while he has been nearly hidden among the crowd during his life, and has at last died, solitary and in sorrow, in a foreign land.

It is at all times difficult, if not impossible, to argue others into a love of poets and poetry: it is altogether a matter of feeling, and we must leave to time (while it hallows his memory) to do justice to the reputation of Keats. There were many, however, even among the critics, who held his powers in high estimation; and it was well observed by the Editor of the Edinburgh Review, that there was no other author whatever, whose writings would form so good a test by which to try the love which any one professed to bear towards poetry. In proof of this assertion, we need only refer to the following exquisite Ode, which, that we may do ample justice to the author, we shall quote entire. The poem will be more striking to the reader, when he understands that it was written not long before Mr. Keats left England, when the author's powerful mind had for some time past inhabited a sickened and shaking body,—and had suffered from the baleful effects of the poisoned shafts of *critical malignity*!

Introduced by these striking comments, the lovely Nightingale Ode took on a new poignancy. Doubtless many readers were interested when on September 15, 1822,[27] the *Atheneum* included in a "Necrological Table. For 1821–2" remarks that looked as if they were original:[28]

Keats, John, a young man of distinguished genius as a poet. He died at Rome on the 28th of February, 1821, in the 25th year of his age. . . . [His works are then listed.] Memoirs of his life are announced, to be accompanied with a selection from his unpublished manuscripts, which, when they appear, will be so particularly noticed in this Magazine as to render any further account at this time unnecessary.

Various readers, too, observed in the Philadelphia

reprint of Leigh Hunt's *Foliage*, 1818,[29] among poems
addressed to Shelley, Byron, Moore, Hazlitt, and
others, three sonnets to John Keats. But the majority
of early critics and versifiers knew little or nothing
about the poetry of Keats. He is completely ignored in
the sketches of contemporary English poets J. K. Paul-
ding[30] composed from his reading in 1822. On the contrary, Byron was all the rage. His name and the scan-
dals attached to it were known even by those unfamiliar with his poetry—if they read the magazines or the
American editions of such books as Thomas Medwin's
Journal of the Conversations of Lord Byron (New York,
1824). In Medwin's book they could scarcely have
failed to observe the noble lord's slurs[31] at Keats. Indeed by 1825 "poor Keats" was a sort of legendary, if
unread, versifier.

Two years later that situation came near being
changed, thanks to the efforts of Frederic S. Hill, Boston editor, actor, and playwright. In July, 1827, he had
the clever idea of issuing a series of pamphlets to be
called the *Spirit of Contemporary Poetry*. I have not seen
the original prospectus, but it is discussed in Hill's
monthly magazine, the *Boston Lyceum*, July 15, 1827.[32]
His purpose was to enable Americans to read Coleridge, Barry Cornwall, Keats, Shelley, Croly, Bowles,
Lamb, Henry Neele, and "other gifted spirits of the
same rank, [who] are equally familiar on our lips, and
their literary efforts equally unknown." Each number
was to consist of from thirty to forty-eight octavo

pages. The "first number . . . just issued" contains selections from the *Sibylline Leaves,* the second further poems of Coleridge, and the third choice pieces by Barry Cornwall,[33] whose poems were later extended through a fourth. The four parts, bound in paper covers as a book with continuous pagination[34] and described on the title-page as "Number I,"[35] brought Hill's laudable scheme to an end. Even this one volume was a drug on the market. In his *New-England Galaxy, and Boston Mercury,* September 11, 1829, he advertises for sale at the *Galaxy* office "a few complete sets in four numbers of the Spirit of Contemporary Poetry, Vol. I. American Edition." Originally sold at fifty cents a number (or two dollars a volume), they can now be bought "at a large discount." The advertisement was often repeated, as on October 23, 30, November 6, 13, 27, December 18, 25, 1829, and January 29, 1830. Then its form was changed to *Select Poems from the Works of Coleridge. . . . Also, The following Poems by Barry Cornwall . . .* on February 12. Still other forms —as Coleridge's poems and Cornwall's poems separately—were used, sometimes two or three in the same issue of the *Galaxy,* up to October 15, 1830. Evidently Hill had considerable difficulty in selling, even at a discount, all the printed copies.

Meanwhile, John Neal had spent three years (1824–1827) in the British Isles as a contributor to *Blackwood's.* He could hardly have failed to learn something about Keats' life and work, especially since he once met Leigh Hunt, whom he greatly admired. Back in Portland, Maine, Neal began to edit the *Yankee,* and his brief note of January 16, 1828,[36] on Keats was obviously indebted to Lockhart's *Blackwood's* comments[37] on Keats and the Cockney School.

IMMORTALITY.

We know of nothing more beautiful or more affecting than the idea below, for the epitaph of a young poet;—and we press it upon the sober consideration of all who are addicted to poetry; assuring them . . . that if they are nothing more than poets in this world, their epitaphs will indeed be *writ in water. . . .*

Poor Keates, who made some delightful poetry in the course of a short life, and died of a broken heart—or properly speaking of the Reviewers; threw up a respectable trade (he was an apothecary's apprentice) and took to scribbling, in the hope of something more than he obtained—a few weeks notoriety, in a small neighborhood. Yet he was a highly gifted young man; of that we have unquestionable proof in the fact, that he was the familiar friend of Leigh Hunt, of Hazlitt and of Shelly.

Shelley's vogue was as belated as that of Keats: the works of both, unprinted in America, were difficult to come by. Hence Neal was delighted when an "unknown" correspondent sent him a copy of Shelley's "Hymn to Intellectual Beauty"—"we had never seen it before"—which he printed in the *Yankee,* April 23, 1828.[38] Like many others, he was fascinated by Hunt's *Lord Byron and Some of His Contemporaries* (London,

1828), a book George Keats had read with disapproval in Louisville[39] before May 12, 1828. Reviewing it enthusiastically in the *Yankee*, May 21, 1828,[40] Neal refers to Shelley and Keats as "these wonderful young men," and confesses that he would like to write "a good long paper about Leigh Hunt, about Byron, about Shelley, and about poor Keats," but lacks space for it.

Remarkably enough, one P. P. in July, 1828, daringly prophesied of Shelley: "The school to which he belonged, or rather which he established, can never become popular. His poems will probably be read for some time by scholars, but even they will eventually neglect them."[41] Yet in the same journal, September 15,[42] Keats is sympathetically treated by its editor, the poet Sumner Fairfield, among "The Young Poets of Britain." Fairfield, who had met Campbell, Coleridge, and other poets during his visit to England in 1826,[43] later appended this material to *Abaddon, The Spirit of Destruction* (New York, 1830).[44] I assume that his remarks are original (it would be too bad if so savage a complainer about Bulwer-Lytton's plagiarism from *him* should be a plagiarist), although his tone and occasionally his phraseology remind one of the account of the *Lamia* volume in the *London Magazine*, September, 1820.[45] They run as follows:

The beautiful skies of literature are often darkened by storms of passion, interest and revenge, but the annals of letters cannot record a more fearful sacrifice to the unprin-

12

cipled vengeance of party,[46] than the fine-minded and unfortunate Keats. His pure spirit allied itself to the kindred mind of Shelley, without imbibing contamination from his principles. His heart was ever reaching after a purer state of morals and society, but he did not scorn or offend the institutions of existing polity. The dim genius of antiquity hovered over his thoughts, and he basked in the imaginative glories of forgotten days. He shrunk from the follies and crimes around him, and sought refuge from their influence in the dreams and oracles of other years, yet, while he revived the beautiful and majestic imaginings of the olden time, and laboured to inculcate their high doctrines upon modern degeneracy, he was bitterly persecuted by the critical satrap of a mercenary government, who added to the hireling vindictiveness of office, the envy of a low-minded literary rival; and the fine sensibilities of Keats were wantonly sacrificed at the shrine of policy, while Croker exultingly performed the executioner's office.

A proud and dignified independence breathes through all the productions of Keats; but there is nothing in his "Endymion," or "The Eve of St. John [*sic*]," or the unfinished "Hyperion," which could, in any possible degree, justify the privileged virulence of the Quarterly. We can readily believe that high church tories, whose faith reposes on the formulae of obsolete usages, may have found but little entertainment in the writings of this gifted youth; but the bitterness of that undistinguished invective, which they lavished upon him, has, long ago, recoiled upon themselves with tenfold energy. There can be little doubt that the deep distress and despondency which terminated the life of Keats, were primarily occasioned by the relentless persecutions that fol-

13

lowed his writings; and this is not the only instance of premature death, caused by the perfidy and vindictiveness of partisan malevolence, secretly operating through the spirit of literature.

The clear genius of the poet was clouded, and his spirit broken down by the infinite contumelies of his enemies. The demon of party snatched him from his studies, arrested his composition of "Hyperion," and banished him to the continent; there he lingered awhile, and then departed to a happier world, in the flower of his youth, and vigour of his hopes. The savage decree of his foes was fulfilled—the sacrifice was performed, but woe be to those who personated the high priests of the fiendish rites! Let the poet be judged by himself. What can be more distinct, beautiful, and true, than this address to the nightingale[47] :—

"Thou wast not born for death, immortal bird! . . ."[48]

Farther on we find a most original and beautiful metaphor, a rare thing; beauty sleeping is

"As though a rose would shut, and be a bud again."

The dethronement of Saturn by Jupiter, forms the subject of Hyperion. How awfully distinct are the images of the poet, as he guides the imagination to the refuge of the fallen god. . . .[49]

He describes Saturn's empress, and then proceeds:—

"How beautiful if sorrow had not made. . . ."[50]

Yet the poet who was equal to continued and sustained passages like these, fell a victim to the cold-blooded atrocity of a cringing office-holder, to the malignity and envy of Croker, Secretary to the Admiralty.[51] So long as literature

14

and the fine arts are made the vehicles of political and re-
ligious intolerance and calumny—so long as genius is sacrificed on the altar of Belial and Mammon—so long as personal animosity guides the pen of the public reviewer, the
difficulties to be surmounted, the trials to be borne, and the
dangers to be resisted in the pathway of poetry, will deter
most men of genius and sensibility from the conflict. They
will be more disposed to leave the gory arena to the Quarterly gladiators alone, and seek, in the bosom of retirement,
that quiet happiness which seldom visited the heart of the
unhappy Keats.

Fairfield was evidently proud of these unimportant
comments. He used them again in a series of "Poetical
Portraits" (Coleridge being added) in his *North American Magazine*, Philadelphia, September, 1833.[52]

Although S. L. Knapp, in his *Lectures on American
Literature* (New York, 1829),[53] failed to list Keats along
with Southey, Scott, Byron, Coleridge, "the polished
Campbell," and others who had made the nineteenth
century "an age of poetry," a turning point in Keats'
vogue came in August, 1829. F. S. Hill had made a failure not only with the *Spirit of Contemporary Poetry* but
also with the *Specimens of American Poetry* S. G. Good-
rich had picked him to edit. Both tasks were carried
out by his Cambridge friend, Samuel Kettell.[54] The
Specimens duly appeared under his editorship in three
volumes (Boston, 1829); the *Spirit* he carried on in his
weekly paper, the *Boston Mercury*. Unluckily no copy
of that paper has been accessible to me, but its literary

contributions are described by N. P. Willis and Kettell himself in other journals.

At this time Willis, a recent graduate of Yale, was editing the Boston *American Monthly Magazine*. He and Kettell and Hill were intimately associated, and their roles in making Keats known to the East can scarcely be overemphasized. Kettell (or possibly Hill) said of Willis, September 25, 1829:[55] "It has been our custom to write pretty paragraphs about him and his poetry since the day that he first commenced author; and in us he has had both a champion and a trumpeter." Later on, Hill consistently praised Willis' magazine, though occasionally[56] reproving his lapses of taste.

In the *American Monthly Magazine*, August, 1829,[57] Willis pays his compliments to Kettell's new journalistic venture:

There are lying before us three or four numbers of the "Mercury," a daintily printed paper, edited (the secret is out) by Kettell the compiler of Specimens of American Poetry. Mr. K. is a scholar, and a "ripe and rare one," with a taste for the *bijouterie* of literature which will cover the talaria of Mercury with gems of the first water. The numbers already published contain several of our pet scraps—things we have copied till our fingers ached from thumbed manuscripts and choice books. It is not every-body, for instance that has got a copy of Keats's "Lamia," and the "Eve of St. Agnes," and here they are printed as if for a lady's sofa reading, on the fairest of type and paper. This praise is generous of us, for our rarities will no longer be rare.

16

The *Boston Mercury*, then, before August 22, 1829, made accessible the texts of at least two great poems. One of them Kettell provided with a critical and biographical notice which G. P. Morris thought of well enough to reproduce in his *New-York Mirror, and Ladies' Literary Gazette*.[58] The notice, as Morris failed to recognize, is borrowed with a few verbal changes and additions from the *London Magazine* essay that *Time's Telescope* had reprinted in 1822.[59]

Hill bought control of the weekly *New-England Galaxy* and of the *Boston Mercury* in this same month. The first issue of his combined *New-England Galaxy, and Boston Mercury*, September 4, 1829, announces: "In uniting the Mercury with the Galaxy, he [Hill] secures the services of Mr. S. KETTELL, and hopes that much advantage will be derived from the arrangement." Hill says also that his own time is largely taken up by other editorial duties, though he hopes "to be of some assistance in the preparation of material" for the *Galaxy*. That Kettell was mainly in control is to be inferred from the reprint in this first issue[60] of the "Hymn to Pan" from *Endymion* and of "Robin Hood." In the next issue (September 11) Kettell makes it quite clear that his *Boston Mercury* had merely attempted to carry on Hill's abortive *Spirit of Contemporary Poetry*. Under the heading "Contemporary Poetry" he remarks:

A series of articles under this title was commenced in the columns of the Mercury, with the first number of that paper, and was received with general approbation. The object in compiling these numbers was, to present some choice extracts from the works of several of the modern British poets but little known in this country, but whose writings had entitled them to remembrance among the master-spirits of the literature of the present age. The plan, indeed, was like that of a periodical published in this city two years ago, called "The Spirit of Contemporary Poetry," and so far as the columns of a weekly print would allow, it was intended that these selections should serve as a continuation of that periodical.

On September 25 Kettell published the following excellent critique, the first of any real merit to be compiled about Keats by an American. Here he makes still further changes in the old *London Magazine* article he had used in the *Boston Mercury,* and to it adds from some English source overlooked by me a fine introduction of two paragraphs as well as a concluding paragraph which may, or may not, be of his own composition. The article is worth giving in full for the light it throws on Kettell's methods.[61]

CONTEMPORARY POETRY.

"The Eve of St. Agnes" we regard as one of the richest and most beautiful poems to be found in the English language. Rich in the new, the remarkable and yet the perfectly natural imagery with which it is crowded,—beautiful in the gentleness of sentiment and the melody of language that characterize its every stanza.

We do not mean to say that we look upon it as a faultless production. It came from the heart of one too youthful, and too enthusiastic and too full of those "burning thoughts that

18

will not brook restraint," to be free from errors and indications of a judgment hardly arrived at its maturity. It requires no critical acumen to run over its lines, and to designate phrases which savour of affectation, and ideas feebly conceived and quaintly or meanly expressed. These however cannot dwell long in the mind of the reader who will but mark with what ease the author conjures up a train of splendid shapes, and with what effect he causes them to pass by, like the shadows of a pleasant dream, or the shifting hues of a summer sunset. The "tiger-moth's deep-damask'd wings," which he spreads over his blazonry; the "carved angels" on the cornice,

"With hair blown back, and wings put cross-ways[62] on their breasts,"

the moonlit casement, "high and triple-arched," blushing "with blood of kings and queens," and the lustrous salvers gleaming in the dim, silvery twilight,—are figures which will haunt the brain in colors too vivid, and in forms too palpable, ever to be forgotten.[63]

Mr. Keats was, in the truest sense of the word, *a poet.* Unfortunately for his fame but[64] a small portion of the public is[65] acquainted with his writings[66]; and yet they are replete with delicate imaginations, full of originality, and eloquent with the sweetest music.[67] During the early part of his career, he was almost concealed among the common crowd, until Envy singled him out, and busied herself in the work of defaming his spotless character, and Malice exposed him to the sneers and jibes of the unfeeling.[68] He died at last[69] solitary and in sorrow, in a foreign land.

It is at all times difficult, if not impossible, to argue others into a love of poets and poetry; it is altogether a matter of feeling, and it must be left[70] to time, while it hallows his memory, to do justice to the reputation of Keats. There were some[71] who held his powers in high estimation; and it was well observed in the[72] Edinburgh Review, that there was no author[73] whose writings would form so good a test as his,[74] by which to try the relish that[75] any one professed for[76] poetry.

When Keats left England, he had a presentiment that he should not return to the land of his nativity.[77] After his arrival in Italy, he revived for a[78] period, but soon afterwards declined and sunk gradually into the[79] grave. He was one of the three English poets who had been compelled by adverse[80] circumstances to adopt a foreign country as their home.[81] Of these Byron was proud to hail him as one of the chosen sons of Apollo, and Shelley died with a volume of his poems pressed to his bosom. When shall we see the places of these filled by men worthy to be remembered as they are?—Keats was the youngest of these brothers in soul, and the first to depart.[82] His sad and beautiful wish was[83] accomplished: It was that he might drink "of the warm South," and "leave the world unseen," and—(he is addressing the nightingale,)

"And with thee fade away into the forest dim:
Fade far away, dissolve, and quite forget. . . ."[84]

A few weeks before he died, a gentleman who was sitting by his bed-side, spoke of an inscription to his memory; but he declined this altogether,—desiring that there should be no mention of his name or country; "or if any," said he, "let it be—*Here lies the body of one, whose name was writ in water!*"[85]

But enough of this melancholy subject. Let us no more

think of him as one of the departed, but fancy that we see him in his exquisite pieces of workmanship. These it may one day be our task to collect. That they are worthy of preservation among the choicest morsels of English poetry, let the "Eve of St. Agnes" bear witness.

"The Eve of St. Agnes" is then printed in full, a circumstance that makes Kettell's borrowings or plagiarisms seem comparatively venial. It is perhaps hazardous to assume that the conclusion, with its threat to edit Keats, was written by Kettell; yet undoubtedly he had access to first editions of Keats' poems. Original criticism was beyond his capacity, but he was a good compiler, a fair editor, and for 1829 he could have executed the plan (if it *was* his) well enough.

The "ethics" of Kettell are none too clear. When in his "Contemporary Poetry" column for September 11, 1829, the subject was Barry Cornwall, he not only mentioned his source, the *Edinburgh Review*, but also used quotation marks. Again, his October 2 article on Shelley and *Prometheus Unbound* begins with quotation marks, thus:

"Mr. Shelley's style, says the Edinburgh Review, is to poetry. . . ."

Quotation marks also conclude the extracts he takes from that *Review*,[86] but there is nothing even to intimate that the remainder of the article is borrowed from *Blackwood's Edinburgh Magazine*.[87] Then on November 6 he printed a long criticism of *The Revolt of Islam*

21

which likewise makes no acknowledgment of any sort about its copying of *Blackwood's*.[88] In all his borrowed material he made verbal changes and omitted words, sentences, or paragraphs at will.

Whether Kettell was deliberately plagiarizing, or merely carrying too far the habit of his day in the use of English periodicals, is not wholly clear; but readers of the *Galaxy* on October 16 (or today) were (and are) likely to be deceived by the long essay on *Endymion*. It begins, "We had never happened to see either of Keats's volumes till very lately," and we "have been exceedingly struck with the genius they display, and the spirit of poetry which breathes through all their extravagance." The natural inference would be that Kettell had just read (as indeed he had!) the 1818 and 1820 poems, and that he was giving his own reactions. Yet surely the *Edinburgh Review* was too well known in America to be plagiarized with any hope of success. It seems likely that when Lord Jeffrey's famous remarks on *Endymion*[89] were reproduced without credit in the *Galaxy* of October 16, Kettell was making no deliberate attempt at deception. His reprint, which runs to three columns on two pages, is striking to look at.[90] If it gave unwary readers a false impression of Kettell's critical powers, it also provided an excellent account of the merits and defects of *Endymion* as well as the text of the poem "Fancy."

Perhaps it was Kettell's reprints that made Willis complain in January, 1830,[91] just after the Paris edition of Keats had been published, of the difficulty Americans had in finding the poems of Keats and Shelley. For that reason, he said truly, "without half of Shelley's power, . . . [Alaric Watts] is more known and quoted—without half of Keats's grace and fervor he has twice his fame." Towards the end of the year Willis managed for the first time to read *Adonais* in the album of a friend who had transcribed it in England, and he printed extracts.[92] Keats, he remarks, was "a spirit more finely constructed, perhaps, even than . . . [Shelley's] own." "We have long been trying unsuccessfully to get a volume of Keats's Poems," he continues, "and when we do succeed we shall endeavor to express our feelings in reference to his genius and his fate more fully than we dare now." If Keats was hard to buy in literary Boston, what must the case have been elsewhere in America? Yet, because of Kettell's activity, there was no excuse for George B. Cheever's omitting Keats from *Studies in Poetry* (Boston, 1830), while Shelley and the other Romantics were included. The *New-England Galaxy*, for that matter, had agents in three Massachusetts cities besides Boston, in three other New England states, in New York, Baltimore, Philadelphia, Washington, D.C., and in Savannah and Natchez. By November 12, 1830, it had, Hill says, 3000 subscribers, more, he thinks, than any other New England newspaper. Its readers were more or less familiar with Keats' life and work, and Cheever's ignorance seems unpardonable. In his "book of practical poetical rhetoric" he advises young ladies and others that Wordsworth, Coleridge, and Campbell are "to be *studied*," while the second-class poets, "such as Rogers, Scott, Grahame &c" are to be "perused with benefit and pleasure." No doubt Keats, if included, would have gone with Shelley in the "&c."

On April 30, 1830, *Boston Mercury* appeared for the last time in the title of the *Galaxy*. The May 7 number is called the *New-England Galaxy, A Weekly Epitome of News, Literature, and the Arts*, Hill is described as "editor and proprietor," and presumably Kettell's connection with the weekly had come to an end. On August 20, 1830, Hill, in spite of his earlier failure with the *Spirit of Contemporary Poetry*, got out a prospectus for *Specimens of the Modern English Poets*.[93] He now proposes to print "in a compact and cheap form" specimens, with biographical sketches, from seventeen poets, including Wordsworth, Southey, Crabbe, Montgomery, Hunt, Lamb, Wilson. Each volume is to have about one hundred double-column pages. The first number, to include Coleridge and Croly, will be published early in September, 1830; the second, with Shelley, Hunt, Keats, and Cornwall, and the four or six other numbers will appear at six-week intervals. Modeled on John Aikin's *Select Works of the British Poets* (two volumes, 1820), each number will sell for seventy-five cents. Hill is circulating the prospectus widely since "nothing but an extensive sale will cover the expenses of publication." This advertisement is repeated

24

in the *Galaxy* for September 3, 10, 24; then on October 1 the date of the Coleridge-Croly number is advanced to October, 1830; while on October 8 and 15 the price of each number is raised to a dollar. This worthy scheme, too, came to nothing. Hill fell into serious financial difficulties, and lost control of the *Galaxy*.[94] Very soon copies of the Paris edition of Coleridge, Shelley, and Keats reached Boston, further undermining his scheme. But Hill, like Kettell, deserves well of students for his persistent efforts at making the contemporary British poets readily accessible to Americans.

II

IN ENGLAND "so small was the demand for Keats's poetry that no separate reprint of it was called for till nearly twenty years after his death"[1]—in 1840. As late as January 9, 1835, John Taylor wrote: "I should like to print a complete Edition of Keats's Poems, with several of his Letters, but the world cares nothing for him—I fear that even 250 copies would not sell."[2] Charles Brown in 1837 had similar fears.[3] Severn's opinion was different. He told Brown on August 21, 1838: "Keats stands so high with all the aspiring young men, particularly the aristocrats, that a book [of his poems] would take."[4] Meanwhile the poems of Keats had "taken" a number of times in America. His reputation was increasing every day among "aristocratic" college students, critics, and ordinary readers on the Eastern seaboard. Severn's impressionistic judgment, "in America he [Keats] has always had a solid fame, independent of the old English prejudices,"[5] is not far from the truth.

The credit for much of Keats' early popularity belongs to a composite, unauthorized edition, *The Poetical Works of Coleridge, Shelley, and Keats. Complete in*

One Volume, issued at Paris in December,[6] 1829, by A. and W. Galignani, who in a "notice" correctly informed readers that "the present edition of the Works of Coleridge, Shelley, and Keats, is infinitely more perfect than any of those published in London; as they have been favoured, from private sources, with many original productions of these esteemed writers, which are now for the first time given to the public."[7] The book—which sold for 25, 35, and 60 francs, according to the paper on which it was printed—is said[8] to have been edited by the journalist Cyrus Redding. If so, in his memoir of Keats he did little but summarize the account given in Hunt's *Lord Byron and Some of His Contemporaries* (1828).[9] "The short career of JOHN KEATS was marked by the development of powers which have been rarely exhibited in one at so immatured an age," "a genius of a lofty and novel order." Much is told of how the *Quarterly* reviewer "is supposed to have hastened his end, which was slowly approaching when the criticism before-mentioned appeared"; and Gifford is attacked by name. In Keats' verse "there are sparkling gems of the first lustre everywhere to be found." "Keats was, as a poet, like a rich fruit-tree which the gardener has not pruned of its luxuriance. . . ."

The Galignani volume, though barred from England as a piracy, established firmly Keats' and Shelley's, and greatly helped Coleridge's, American reputation. One Harvard student tells that he ordered a copy direct

27

from Paris.[10] It and other piracies by the same firm were quickly imported and advertised by American booksellers. George Keats wrote Dilke on November 22, 1830, that he had seen a new life of his brother announced: "I now hear that the work is for sale in the eastern Cities and have sent for a copy: the volume advertised contains 'Shelly, Colridge and Keats poems.' " It was on sale in Boston about this time. On December 10 Hill[11] editorially announced:

A splendid French Edition of the Poetical Works of Coleridge, Shelley and Keats, complete in one volume, imperial Octavo, is hereby offered for a suitable NEW YEAR'S ADDRESS, for the carriers of the New-England Galaxy. Contributions may be addressed to the editor, until the 15th instant.

Likewise in December,[12] Willis remarked:

Those of our readers who lounge at the booksellers' shops, have admired the beautiful quarto editions of the contemporary poets, lately imported from France. . . . Two volumes lie beside us—one of which contains the works of Coleridge, Shelley and Keats, with beautiful portraits of these authors, and the other, those of Milman, Bowles, Barry Cornwall and Wilson, also with portraits.

The cost of Paris publication, he added, is only one-sixth of that in London, and accordingly "we get them in this country far cheaper than we could print them." Six months later Willis complained:[13] "Some one has borrowed our Galignani Edition of Keats. We take this opportunity to advertise it, and request the borrower to return it as soon as he may make it convenient." Continuing the advertisement, he reprinted the Nightingale Ode.

The Galignani volume was in turn pirated in America, where various composite editions of Keats, reprinted or imitated from it (but overlooked by his biographers and bibliographers), show clearly that in the decade from 1830 to 1840 he was much better known and more highly esteemed by the general reading public of the East than by that of Great Britain. The first reprint I have seen, "Stereotyped by J. Howe," and—though in one issue bearing no name—published by John Grigg, was issued at Philadelphia in 1831 and again in 1832 as *The Poetical Works of Coleridge, Shelley, and Keats, Complete in One Volume*.[14] Grigg, who set up his own firm in 1823, soon had "what was probably the largest book distributing house in the world."[15] How far inland his Keats volume penetrated is hard to tell. Mr. R. L. Rusk[16] finds no mention of works by Keats, Coleridge, Shelley, and Wordsworth "in the forty-page list of books advertised by one of the chief Ohio booksellers in 1831"; but he does note that a Coleridge-Shelley-Keats volume was in the Ohio State Library in 1832 and in libraries at Kenyon College in 1834, Miami University in 1835, and the Cincinnati Mercantile Association by 1838. "The vogue of the three . . ., small as it was," he remarks, "was due in part to the fact that all of these poets were early to be had together in a single volume." Howe's stereotyped volume was reissued under the name of Desilver, Thomas, and Company, Philadelphia, first in 1835 and then in 1836 and 1837, and again by Thomas, Cowperthwait, and Company, Philadelphia, in 1838 and 1839.[17]

Timothy Flint commented in 1835[18] on how American publishers "favour the circulation of English works, which they could publish without leave of the author," Harper of New York publishing "six English books, to one of American origin," and on how American readers have "a deep and innate preference" for English books. As a result, Americans unfamiliar with any one of the Coleridge-Shelley-Keats volumes could have become acquainted with Keats in American reprints of various English books. For example, in the New York issue, 1831, of the Reverend George Croly's *The Beauties of the British Poets*, Keats has more space[19] than Coleridge, Southey, or Wordsworth—and Shelley is omitted. To be sure, Croly's language[20] is somewhat restrained:

Keats died at an early age, probably long before his powers were matured; but not till he had given promise of excellence in his peculiar style. His versification was chiefly formed on the model of Spenser; and few as his poems are, they exhibit a rich and delicate conception of the beauty of our language.

Again, readers of Moore's *Letters and Journals of Lord Byron* (New York, 1830–31) or its reviews observed that, as Willis[21] puts it, "Byron did not like Keats";

30

and those who turned to E. J. Trelawny's *Adventures of a Younger Son* (New York, 1832)[22] must have noticed that—to quote Charles Brown—"at the head of every chapter are one or two quotations from Byron, Keats, and Shelley,—from *no one else*." There were, said Brown (who supplied them), fifty-three quotations, some previously unpublished, from Keats; and he thought "that these quotations, in so popular a book, will be of great service to the fame of Keats."[23] Brown was right. A review published in Boston, January, 1833,[24] said:

The mottoes of every chapter are, without exception, from one of three authors, Byron, Shelley, or Keats. Trelawney was the friend and favorite of each of these gifted men; and it is possible that previous to his acquaintance with them in Italy, he had read little. . . . He has at any rate exhibited his taste in the selection of these fragments from the remains of his departed companions; and it is singular to observe how remarkably the imaginations of each in their kind had shadowed forth scenes and images of a kindred spirit with those which it has been the fate of their more muscular friend to see and struggle in.

Just as Smith's Standard Library, London, was reprinting (from the Galignanis) a separate volume called *The Poetical Works of John Keats,* 1840, 1841, the Philadelphia firm of Thomas, Cowperthwait, and Company got out another hybrid collection, unmentioned by Colvin, Miss Lowell, and the rest: *The Poetical Works of Howitt, Milman, and Keats, Complete in One Volume,*

31

1840. It, too, is an imitation of the Galignani Coleridge-Shelley-Keats of 1829, from which the memoir and poems of Keats are taken. The 1840 preface remarks: "The many editions already published of Keats's works have sufficiently attested his popularity. His reputation has been continually advancing since the period of his lamented death." Perhaps only imitation and tradition kept the publishers from issuing Keats in a separate volume, or perhaps they wished to increase their sales by a new compilation to vie with the old Coleridge-Shelley-Keats volume.[25] The editor's preface further says:

In selecting from among the recent poets of Great Britain two, whose works had not been hitherto presented collectively to the American reader, to be published with a new edition of Keats, it was, of course, his object to give the preference to those which would be most acceptable to the public—most popular. He chose Mary Howitt and Henry Hart Milman.

Mrs. Howitt, the author of some one hundred ten works, should have been immortalized by this association, but her name is unmentioned by Keats' formal biographers, and her own autobiography contains no indication that she was aware of her American vogue—from which she derived fame but no money.

After 1840 the two Philadelphia volumes were occasionally reissued: the new Howitt-Milman-Keats by Crissy and Markley in 1846, 1847, 1849, and 1852; the old Coleridge-Shelley-Keats by Thomas, Cowper-

32

thwait in 1844 and by Crissy and Markley in 1847. Then following the London editions, Wiley and Putnam, of New York, published Keats' poems separately in 1846 and 1847.[26]

In copies of the Philadelphia editions which I have seen—and there may well have been other reprints—various owners' names, or bookplates, appear. These early lovers, or at any rate buyers, of Keats deserve the tribute of reproduction: John A. Baker; G. H. Deane; Francis W. Garrettson; Fred S. Gossler, 1838; H. S. Haines; John Home; S. E. Howard; F. Lawrence, 1832 (sold by J. L. Hosford, Albany, New York); Spencer and Kate E. Linnell, Canandaigua, New York; Caroline Scholl Rhinebeck; W. G. Sergeant; Frances W. Swan; Hannah Swan, 1849; Thomas Ward; and G. G. Williams. Wiley and Putnam editions seen by me were owned by S. G. Driscol and Isaac B. Tompkins, Jr., of New Bedford, Massachusetts; Alberta Tobb; and Maria F. Wheeler. If all these persons could be identified, new light would be thrown on the geographical extent of the poet's reputation.

III

THE VOGUE of Keats is largely a tale of five or six cities. It originated mainly in the Philadelphia editions of his poems; it was fostered throughout the East, especially by the periodicals of Philadelphia and New York, by Willis, Kettell, and Hill in Boston, and by a whole group of Harvard undergraduates in Cambridge. Partly by the last, Keats' fame was transplanted to Louisville, Kentucky, and in some slight degree to the Southwest. All along, the cemetery in the Eternal City drew sentimental travelers from many states. "Poor Keats" quickly became a legend.

Willis' contribution has already been stressed. No other American did more than he to build the poet's reputation, and everybody who read the *American Monthly Magazine* attentively came to expect references to Keats and reprints of his verse. One "A.," in November, 1830,[1] attacking "the illiberality of the daily Press," concluded:

If it is not either crushed or corrected, we shall soon have among us that savage system of bullying which destroyed the fine fancy and powerful invention of poor Keats, and which was pursued from no angry passion, but on a cold-blooded mercenary calculation of the profits which idle curiosity, and the appetite for slander, might enable its authors to derive from it.

Important, too, was Albert Pike, who left Boston in 1831 and became known as the "Arkansas Poet." In his "Autobiography"[2] he apparently claims to have done "two years' work in one at Harvard"[3] about 1830, but his words were either thoughtlessly written or else have been misinterpreted. On March 17, 1890, he wrote from Washington, D.C., to W. H. Tillinghast, compiler of the Quinquennial Catalog:

> I am not a graduate of Harvard. I passed examinations successfully for the purpose of entering, in 1825, presented myself a year afterward for the purpose of entering the Junior Class, having completed the Freshman and Sophomore studies during the year at home; declined to pay the *two* years tuition required of me; and so never was a student for even a day, at the University.[4]

Through his close association with Willis, Pike rapidly developed an enthusiasm for Keats that the Galignani volume strengthened. His "Hymns to the Gods," composed in 1829–1830,[5] published in Willis' *American Monthly Magazine*,[6] and republished in *Blackwood's Edinburgh Magazine*,[7] have been called, says Miss Riley,[8] "the most clever imitations of Keats's 'Hymn to Pan' in *Endymion* that probably any mortal has ever written," though they are original "in adapting further material to the pattern set by his master." Pike's early familiarity with Keats is unquestionable. He contrib-

35

uted to the *American Monthly Magazine*[9] in 1829–1830
"The Progress of Poetry," where Keats is featured as
one of ten "living poets" (Byron, Scott, Coleridge,
Shelley, Wordsworth, Moore, Campbell, Southey,
Crabbe) thus:

> And there was one with a wilder look,
>   Like the light of a dying eye;
> And a rain of golden mist he shook,
>   As he wandered about the sky:
> He loved the quiet woods, and there
>   He would stay and sleep for hours,
> Like a sun-drop hung in the middle air,
>   And blinding the birds with its showers,
> And sounding a music most low and sweet,
> On every leaf that it chanced to meet.

For the same journal, January, 1831,[10] he wrote an essay on "The Philosophy of Bowling," imagining that
he saw Byron, Coleridge, Croly, Crabbe, and Wordsworth among bowlers. In addition to them, "Keats—
blessings on his spirit, whether it be in air or earth—
must have rolled a curve, with a quiet, slumbering mo-
tion. Shelley, a fiery, bounding ball, with an eye like
an eagle's following it." More striking still, to Charles
Dingley's New York *Euterpeiad*, April 1, 1831,[11] Pike
contributed the following poetic tribute to his early
master.

SONNET TO KEATS.

Oh thou most patient-ey'd and meek and mild!
Thou that do'st live in every wave *that smiled;*

In every leaf that rustled with a hymn—
In every stream, and dell, and forest wild—
In every thing abounding with a dim
And secret beauty;—thou who didst enthrone,
Amid the fire of thy rich heart, each god
Of old Mythology; and, all alone,
Didst offer them thy deep and springing flood
And incense of pure song: Oh thou sick heart!
Weeping thyself away like evening dew,
For scorn, and curled lip, and sneering tone;
Still, like the woods and fields, and mountains blue,
Shall human souls ring henceforth to thy heart.

Say—whither went thy soul at feel of death?
Out to the west where patient sunset rode
Amid thick bars of gold, upon a breath
Of brilliant vapor? else where sunrise strode
With flame upon his brow? or where the fire
From moon and star, had built upon white cloud
Streaming pavilions?—where the leaves had showed
By night upon the earth?—where the great lyre
Of the blue sea was sounding, with a might
Of deep, sweet harmony—where the mist invests
Some fountain, drifted through the dun twilight
Of mountain shades—or where the constant song
Of fiery drifts was in the northern sky?
In some great beauty thou art even at rest,
Dreaming, awake—with ever patient eye.

A. P.

When Pike's *Prose Sketches and Poems* was published in 1834, it was much talked about and, says the

Boston Pearl,[12] false hints are everywhere "thrown out that we are about to find a Keats and Shelley and Coleridge combined." The style, said a *New-England Magazine*[13] reviewer, "reminds one of Shelley, indeed; and, here and there, of Keats." He was correct. "The Lightning,"[14] for instance, is a mere rewriting of Shelley's "Cloud" with all its poetry missing. But Keatsian influence on Pike is manifested more in his early poems that clutter the magazines than in those, except the "Hymns," yet collected.

Even more influential as Keats disciples were James Freeman Clarke and Samuel Osgood. Clarke, who was graduated from Harvard College in 1829 and from the Divinity School in 1833, went to considerable trouble and expense to buy the 1829 Paris Coleridge-Shelley-Keats volume. In June, 1865, he gave to a daughter his copy, in which he penned the following note:

> This book I bought in 1830, when I was twenty years old. . . . I was poor, and it was a good deal to me to pay $7.50 for a book. But the American edition of this work had not then been published, nor had there been then printed, even in England, a complete edition of either of these poets. So I imported a copy of this Paris edition, and had a great deal of pleasure out of it.

During the winter of 1830–1831, late at night, "I would read awhile in this book, and I hope that you may have as much pleasure out of it as I had then."[15] Samuel Osgood, now less well known than Clarke, was a transcendentalist, a voluminous author, and long-time pastor of the New York Church of the Messiah. From Harvard he received the degrees of A.B., 1832, B.D., 1835, honorary S.T.D., 1855. Writing to Lord Houghton on November 26, 1875, he boasted that Keats' "poems were the delight & wonder of our little reading coterie at Harvard University so long ago."

The "little coterie" included many afterwards famous and influential men, among them Clarke, Unitarian minister, transcendentalist, prolific writer; Charles Timothy Brooks, poet and translator; John Sullivan Dwight, class poet, later a literary and music critic; Henry T. Tuckerman, critic and poet; Christopher Pearse Cranch, Unitarian minister, poet, and painter; Thomas Gold Appleton, poet and essayist; John Holmes, younger brother of Oliver Wendell Holmes[16] and intimate friend of James Russell Lowell; Estes Howe, Lowell's brother-in-law, in whose house Arthur Hugh Clough boarded while he was in Cambridge;[17] Henry Whitney Bellows, Unitarian minister, social reformer, and author;[18] George T. Curtis, lawyer and biographer of Webster and Buchanan; John Lothrop Motley, historian and diplomat.[19] Some of these men— Appleton, Bellows, Motley, as well as the poet W. E. Channing and Samuel Gray Ward, mentioned below— had been trained in George Bancroft and Joseph G. Cogswell's fine Round Hill School at Northampton, Massachusetts, which had a library of "about four thousand volumes,"[20] and in its prospectus (June 20, 1823) insisted that "an acquaintance with English lit-

39

erature, must be commenced with the first efforts at learning to read and write the English language. The pupils must be encouraged to grow familiar with our great masters of prose and verse."[21] Both Bancroft and Cogswell were Harvard graduates and former members of the Harvard faculty, the latter as librarian. Bancroft had published his volume of "romantic" *Poems* in 1823, and he was a personal friend of Byron. Small wonder, then, that boys from Round Hill knew their nineteenth-century poets.

At least two members of the "coterie," Appleton and Motley, were contributors to the *American Monthly Magazine*.[22] Willis had complained, August, 1830,[23] of his inability to find a copy of Keats' poems, but in the very next issue he said: "There lies before us now a kind letter, thanking us for our notice of Keats and giving us some passages from his books which we had never before seen . . . if there is anything richer or more beautiful in poetry, we cannot now call it to mind." To prove the statement he quoted from "Isabella" and the "golden, glorious, prodigal profusion" of the Autumn Ode.[24] It seems likely that the "kind letter" was written by Kettell or Appleton or Motley.

In his biography of Motley, Oliver Wendell Holmes tells how the future historian entered Harvard at the age of thirteen, and of how "Shelley was then a great favorite of his."[25] Presumably he also knew Keats, for Appleton[26] says of *Blackwood's*, Motley, and his Harvard circle, "the elegantly brutal onslaughts upon

Whigs and Cockney poets by Christopher North, intoxicated us youths." Osgood himself[27] long remembered "with especial pleasure our evenings with Chaucer and Spenser at Professor Edward T. Channing's study" and "also a little coterie who met to declaim choice pieces of prose and verse with the professor of elocution, our enthusiastic friend, Dr. Barber. Those twelve or fourteen youths have had various destinies," one of them being Motley, "who used to declaim Byron with downturned collar, that showed a throat smooth and full as a girl's."

Jonathan Barber, "Instructer in Elocution," as the 1832 Harvard catalog calls him, deserves no particular notice, but it would be difficult to overestimate the services of E. T. Channing, Boylston Professor of Rhetoric and Oratory—even if John Neal in 1824[28] did say, "There is nothing extraordinary about this man. . . . He should have nothing to do with rhetoric or belles-lettres, except in the way of a concordance, or an index." Harvard men write about him, although he published nothing of importance, in almost smug superlatives. According to T. W. Higginson,[29] Channing "probably trained as many conspicuous authors as all other American instructors put together"; while R. H. Dana, Jr.,[30] asserted:

It is in no spirit of disparagement to other institutions that we refer to the fact, that for the last quarter of a century Cambridge has been distinguished for the purity and elegance of its style in composition and elocution. And it is no injustice to other teachers there, indeed it is but uttering their common voice when we add that the credit of this is chiefly due to Mr. Channing.

But of the romantic poets he preferred "the charm of Scott."

Of the Class of 1832 Osgood[31] remarked: "We were probably more marked for our taste for language and literature, and at last for metaphysics, than for mathematics and exact science." In his Class Oration of July 17 Osgood,[32] who was just twenty, quoted, none too appositely, the famous lines from *Endymion:* "Keats well says:

> 'A thing of beauty is a joy for ever:
> Its loveliness increases: . . .
> Therefore every morrow are we wreathing
> A flowery band to bind us to the earth.'

So may it be, Classmates, with the things that have been pleasant to us here." Keats, at any rate, "remained pleasant" to many Harvard men. Discussing the College as it was in 1834, Edward Everett Hale[33] remarked that among its two hundred fifty students "literature was . . . the fashion," and of the Philadelphia Coleridge-Shelley-Keats that "you saw this book pretty much everywhere." J. R. Lowell[34] bought a copy in that year, but no copy and no verses by the three poets were in the Harvard College Library when it published the *Catalogue* of 1830, while Shelley and Keats were still absent from the 1834 supplement.

Directly after his ordination, Clarke went to Louisville, Kentucky, where he was pastor of a Unitarian church from August 4, 1833, to June 16, 1840.[35] Almost immediately he became acquainted with George Keats, whose memory and virtues he cherished to the end of his days. As early as November, 1834, he wrote to Margaret Fuller:[36] "George Keats is one of the best men in the world. And I have taken a strong liking to the character of his brother John, which has just dawned on me through the medium of his letters and accounts of his personal history." On April 30, 1838, he told Emerson:

My chief companion in the study of Carlyle is Geo. Keats—a brother of the poet John—a merchant of great intelligence & literary taste. . . . He is a man of great energy & activity here, & has built up an estate & influence, without losing a single moral feeling or literary taste. He has kept his literature for the love of it, all alone—for he has had few to sympathize with him.[37]

Osgood presently joined Clarke at Louisville, and was just as favorably impressed by the poet's brother. To Lord Houghton on November 26, 1875, he wrote: "We used to be often together at a Club of the choice men of Louisville Ky.—scholars, men of the learned professions, judges, statesmen &c. There George Keats was well received."[38] These men included Judge John Rowan, lawyer and United States senator, and George D. Prentice, a mediocre poet but a great newspaper editor.

When John Howard Payne visited Louisville in 1834

he was immediately welcomed by the George Keats-Prentice-Rowan-Clarke circle. After twenty years of more or less unfortunate association with the English stage, Payne was now collecting material for a magazine that actually was never published. Under the date of December, 1834, he contributed to the *Ladies' Companion*, New York, August, 1837,[39] an article about his stay in "this most hospitable city." George Keats had shown him various letters and poems written by "the gifted but ill-starred enthusiast," John, which better than anything then in print reveal "his genius and the gentleness and the affectionate earnestness of his feelings." George Keats also "left me, in my Album, a very precious remembrancer, in an inscription of his own, conveying some of these same unpublished treasures." Payne then gave the text of the sonnet, "Fame like a wayward girl," which "cannot be read without emotion by any one who recollects that it was to the unkindness of the awarders of literary fame in England, that the untimely death of the author has been ascribed: that he burst a blood-vessel on reading a savage attack on his 'Endymion' in the London Quarterly Review, and died at Rome of a decline produced in consequence." For good measure he printed part of a letter written by Keats; "A Dream" ("As Hermes once took to his feathers light");[40] a poem beginning "Hither, hither, love,"[41] which he describes as "a literary curiosity" with "wild beauty"; and "A Prophecy" (" 'Tis the witching time of night"), "the most striking, perhaps, among all the productions of their extraordinary author," even though it shows that Keats lacked "knowledge of what rare morceaux our bards have occasionally sent forth to the world."[42]

During 1836–1839 Clarke edited at Louisville the *Western Messenger*, a Unitarian and transcendental journal with decided literary tendencies. Among frequent contributors were Osgood, W. H. Channing, Emerson, J. S. Dwight, C. T. Brooks, and C. P. Cranch, all former students in, and all except Emerson graduates of, the Harvard Divinity School. The general effect it produced was that of a Harvard journal transferred to the blue grass. Because of his deep-rooted love for Keats' poetry and his respect for George Keats, Clarke, in June and July, 1836,[43] printed two letters of the poet to his brother Tom as well as the ode "To Apollo" ("God of the golden bow").[44] Clarke wrote:[45]

The poetical writings of this young author are fresh and living in the hearts of the lovers of poetry in this country and Europe. They have the genuine *aroma* which denotes the immortalizing presence of genius. They have derived no transient popularity from a fashionable dress, or from sentiments conformed to the sickly taste of a weak generation, craving for excitement. Keats' style was formed chiefly by a diligent study of the old English poets, especially of Spenser. It is an entire mistake to call him a follower of Leigh Hunt. He was a follower of no man.

Full details about Keats and the *Western Messenger* have been given by W. H. Venable, in *Beginnings of*

Literary Culture in the Ohio Valley,[46] and by R. L. Rusk, in *The Literature of the Middle Western Frontier*.[47] Keats' recognition in Kentucky, Mr. Rusk believes, "was, it would seem, due to the circumstance of his brother's residence in Louisville and acquaintance with the editor of the *Messenger*. The publication, for the first time, of some of Keats's verse and prose in this magazine marks the point of closest connection between the great English poets and Western periodicals." Without doubt George Keats did everything possible to advance his poet brother's reputation, the growth of which he watched with almost pathetic eagerness. So when in 1837 Lewis J. Cist, bank clerk and poetaster of Cincinnati, asked him for the poet's autograph, he forwarded (June 18) a signature cut from a letter and remarked:

It affords me much gratification to beleive that my brother's genius is becoming more and more highly appreciated—in fact I feel a sort of gratitude towards those who fairly estimate talents that were almost slighted by the public at a time when encouragement might have prolonged the life of a Poet, who had he lived 20 years longer would in my opinion have so enriched english literature, as to have caused his name to be associated by posterity with its greatest.[48]

Indeed, George succeeded so well that the Louisville *Journal*, December 25, 1841, telling of his death on the preceding day, assumed that the poet was known to all its readers: "Mr. Keats was a younger brother of John Keats, the distinguished British poet, and possessed much of the genius, and all of the philosophy, benevolence, and enlarged philanthropy, of the lamented bard."

But Keats' Kentucky fame owed just as much to the fact that Clarke and Osgood and Cranch, leading figures in the exotic *Western Messenger,* "a Boston flower blooming in the Ohio Valley,"[49] had learned to love Keats' poetry before their migration from Cambridge. Mr. Rusk[50] is correct in saying that Clarke "deserves recognition as one of the first critics to realize the value of the poet's prose," and he mentions a eulogistic criticism of Keats in the *Western Monthly Magazine, and Literary Journal,* Cincinnati, May, 1837,[51] which Clarke inspired.

Clarke was assisted as preacher and editor by the transcendentalist Cranch, a graduate of the Harvard Divinity School, 1835, and a close friend of Clarke himself, of Brooks, Osgood, G. W. Curtis, Dwight, Lowell, and John Holmes. Cranch met George Keats in October, 1837, and noted, as others had, that his daughter Emma strongly resembled "Keats, the poet, or that little portrait of him which you see in the volume containing his poems in conjunction with Coleridge and Shelley."[52] In a letter of November 24, 1838, Cranch remarked: "I consider Keats one of the greatest poetical geniuses that for a long time has walked the earth. . . . What might he not have become, had he lived?"[53] Appropriately enough, when he published his *Poems* in 1844, *Graham's Magazine* observed:

47

"Some fine verbal combinations are directly borrowed from Byron, Shelley, Keats and Tennyson. The three latter, with Carlyle, Emerson, Lowell, and a few others, are continually suggested to the mind of the reader."[54]

As Keats' reputation grew, the Protestant Cemetery in Rome with his grave and Shelley's became a Mecca for tourists.[55] Theodore Dwight, a Yale graduate (1814), missed his one chance of immortality by less than three days. He and his family visited the cemetery on the day of Keats' death, February 23, 1821, and were "affected at the sight of a beautiful marble monument" to a Massachusetts woman, Eliza Watson, wife of Sir Grenville Temple.[56] Had he gone after nine on the morning of February 26, he could hardly have failed to mention the new grave of a young English poet. Dr. W. E. Channing also missed a chance when, during the 1822 winter in Rome, he apparently left the graves unvisited and undescribed.[57] Provided by Washington Allston with a letter of introduction to Coleridge, Channing had talked with both Coleridge and Wordsworth in the preceding summer. But "he did not care for Keats . . . perhaps because he was discouraged by the over-sweetness of 'Endymion.' "[58]

It can hardly be denied that even now "poor Keats" owes some of his widespread appeal to his misfortunes, his miserable and early death, and his immortal epitaph. The *New-England Magazine*, December, 1835,[59] was justified in finding "something peculiarly mournful in contemplating the graves and monuments" of the Protestant Cemetery, where "the wild grass which waves over their tombs and conceals their names, is an emblem of the loneliness of their death-bed." As for the inscriptions "they speak to the traveler alone." Americans in the first half of the nineteenth century, like those of our day, felt an irresistible urge to see the Shelley-Keats graves for themselves—and many of them described their emotions in cold print.

One of the earliest, Willis, made his visit during the spring of 1833. In *Pencillings by the Way*[60] he calls Keats "a human victim, sacrificed, not long ago, upon . . . [a] most ruthless altar," and "a poet of very uncommon promise."

He had all the wealth of genius within him, but he had not learned, before he was killed by criticism, the received, and, therefore, the best manner of producing it for the eye of the world. Had he lived longer, the strength and richness which break continually through the affected style of 'Endymion' and 'Lamia' and his other poems, must have formed themselves into some noble monuments of his powers. As it is, there is not a poet living who could surpass the material of his 'Endymion'—a poem, with all its faults, far more full of beauties. But this is not the place for criticism. He is buried fitly for a poet, and sleeps beyond criticism now. Peace to his ashes!

Another, H. T. Tuckerman, who at Harvard had been an especial intimate of H. W. Bellows, lived in Rome during 1833–1834. To the *North American Review*, Boston, April, 1835,[61] he contributed an article on the

49

poet's grave and "the beautiful brilliancy of young genius." The epitaph of "poor Keats" seemed to him totally false:

That name was indeed written in water, but the pencillings of a progressive and discerning spirit could have deepened the inscription upon an adamantine surface of crystal. But what these have failed to do, pity and congeniality are ever doing; and in innumerable hearts the memory of Keats is cherished, with a love surpassing even what the efforts of his mature genius could have inspired.[62]

Still another member of Osgood's Harvard coterie, Appleton,[63] was in Rome during 1834. On March 6 he visited Severn, the young artist who attended Keats in his last moments. . . . There was a portrait of Keats which represented him less thin, though pale, than I had imagined him. . . . I spent several hours with Severn in most agreeable conversation. He told me a thousand things about Keats, and regaled me with choice Falernian, very like claret, a present from a friend of Keats.

Samuel Gray Ward,[64] lifelong friend of Emerson and Margaret Fuller (he says that all his early reading, like that of his associates, "had been of English authors. Miss Edgeworth, Sir Walter Scott, Wordsworth, Southey, Shelley, Keats, Byron, we knew all about"), after his graduation from Harvard in 1836 accompanied John Farrar, Professor of Mathematics, and Mrs. Farrar to England, and some time later went on to Italy. In 1837 he and Professor George Ticknor, of Harvard, for several days traveled with Wordsworth

Season of Mists and mellow fruitfulness
Close bosom friend of the maturing sun;
Conspiring with him how to load and bless
The Vines with fruit that round the thatch eves run.
To bend with apples the mossd Cottage trees
And fill all fruits with sweetness to the core
To swell the gourd, and plump the hazle shells
With a white Kernel; to set budding more
And still more later flowers for the bees
Until they think warm days will never cease
For Summer has o'erbrimm'd their clammy cells

Who hath not seen thee? ~~for thy haunts are many~~ If anyone thy store?
Sometimes whoever seeks ~~for thee~~ abroad may find
Thee sitting ~~careless~~ on a granary floor
Thy hair soft lifted by the winnowing wind
~~While bright the sun slants through the~~ husky barn
~~on on a half reap'd furrow sound asleep~~
~~Or sound asleep in a half reaped field~~
Dosed with red poppies; while thy reaping hook
~~Spares some slumberous~~
~~Spares some minutes while warm slumbers creep~~
Or on a half reap'd furrow sound asleep
Dos'd with the fume of poppies, while thy hook
~~Spares the next swath, and all its twined flowers~~
~~Spares for some slumberous minutes the next swath;~~
And sometimes like a gleaner thou dost keep
Steady thy laden head across the brook.
Or by a Cyder-press with patient look
Thou watchest the last oozing hours by hours

Where are the songs of Spring? Aye where are they?
    Think not of them thou hast thy music too—
While a barred clouds bloom the soft dying day
    And touching the the stubble plains with rosy hue—
Then in a wailful quire the small gnats mourn
    among the river sallows, on the borne aloft
        Or sinking as the light wind lives and dies
    and full grown lambs loud bleat from hilly bou
Hedge crickets sing, and now again full soft
    The Redbreast whistles from a garden croft.
and now flock still
Red of gathering swallows twitter in the Skies—

and Crabb Robinson. The experience, Ward re-marked,[65] "aided me nothing to understand the real Wordsworth better. I wish we had known as little of him, of Shelley, Keats, Coleridge, Byron, as of Shake-speare." At Lucerne, Ward rejoined the Farrars, now accompanied by Mrs. Farrar's cousin, Anna Barker, a young girl whose family had recently moved from Massachusetts to New Orleans. On a subsequent trip to Rome Miss Barker plucked the customary floral trib-ute from the grave of Keats, and some months later gave it to George Keats, to whom in Louisville Clarke introduced her.[66] In gratitude George wrote to Miss Barker, November 15, 1839, enclosing the original manuscript of the "Ode to Autumn," "since you felt interest enough for the memory of my Brother to gather flowers that 'grew over him,' and to preserve them." "The beautiful Miss Barker," whose Greater Boston fame was considerable (Margaret Fuller envied her), married Ward on October 3, 1840.[67]

Keats' memory would probably be kept alive by his tomb if his works were forgotten. Many others of his earliest disciples made pilgrimages to see it. The enor-mously popular hack-writer, J. T. Headley, whose name *was* writ in water, visited the cemetery in April, 1843, and before Keats' monument became entirely maudlin.[68]

I stood alone over this solitary grave of genius and wept. I have read of broken hearts, but nothing ever indicated to me half so lonely and desolate a heart, as the dying language of

Keats. . . . I plucked a flower that was drooping with rain-drops beside the grave and turned away.

Not, however, before composing a poem that reduces Keats' epitaph to absurdity:

> Oh, can one envious tongue
> So blight and blast earth's holiest things,
> That e'en the glorious bard that sings,
> Grows mute—and all unstrung,
> His bleeding, quivering heart gives o'er,
> And dies without one effort more?
>
> 'Tis "writ," as thou hast said,
> Upon the cold gray marble there,
> Each word of that wild, bitter prayer,
> On which thy spirit fled!
> But oh, that injured name is known,
> "Far as the birds of fame have flown."
>
> Yet thou hast said aright,
> Thy name *is* in the water writ,
> *For tears are ever shed on it,*
> Till dims the aching sight,
> By pilgrims from each distant land,
> Who, weeping, round thy grave-stone stand.

A far more sensible description was given by W. M. Gillespie, a Columbia graduate (1834), who later became a distinguished engineer and Union College professor, in *Rome: As Seen by a New-Yorker in 1843–4.*[69] Bayard Taylor's visit was made on January 1, 1846.[70]

Like Shelley he found "a solemn, mournful beauty about the place, . . . that takes away the gloomy associations of death, and makes one wish to lie there, too, when his thread shall be spun to the end." Much more elaborate is the account written by W. I. Kip, Yale graduate (1831) and later Episcopal Bishop of California, in *The Christmas Holydays in Rome* (New York and Philadelphia, 1846).[71] Like Gillespie, he quotes from Shelley's elegy on "poor Keats," and concludes by saying:

Keats will never be forgotten while the English language exists. He was indeed . . . cut off too early to show any maturity of power, but "Endymion," and "Lamia," and "Isabella," are rich in gems of thought, and display on every page the wealth of genius. Shelley's splendid Dirge would alone be sufficient to preserve his memory.

Late in 1846 G. W. Curtis went to Italy with Cranch and Mrs. Cranch, all of whom promptly viewed the Keats-Shelley graves.[72] In a letter to Dwight, November 22, Curtis described the plots where "Shelley and Keats sleep always a summer sleep. Fate is no less delicate than stern, which has here united them after such lives and deaths."[73] Strangely enough, Curtis failed to collect flowers from the grave of Keats to give to Mrs. Whitman.[74] Seven years passed before a Mrs. Allen provided them, and on November 26, 1853, the poetess heartily thanked her for "the flowers from the graves of Keats and Shelley. I have often wished for a single blade of that 'coarse grass' that grows by the grave of

Keats or for a leaf of one of the wild roses that used to bloom by the monument of Shelley." Years later—in 1883—Cranch[75] sent Curtis a poem, "At the Grave of Keats," recollecting in tranquillity their emotions of 1846.

W. E. Channing, the poet, presumably visited the graves, in spite of his distaste for Keats.[76] But in his *Conversations in Rome: Between an Artist, a Catholic, and a Critic* (Boston, 1847)[77] he himself stays quiet, while the others locate Shelley and Keats in the wrong cemeteries. The Artist dislikes the pyramid of Caius Cestius, though he believes "that many Englishmen are attracted to this Pyramid, because there is buried near it one of their men of genius, as I hear,—Shelley." Equally misinformed, the Critic agrees, "His mournful ashes lie in the old Protestant burying-ground, a cold, empty square, surrounded by a formidable trench, and just back of a Powder-magazine. Keats, who is buried near by, in the new burying-ground, is in better quarters." The Artist, unimpressed by *Cor Cordium*, then adds: "What importance, truly, can it be to either of these men, where their mouldering bones are buried? . . . If these two Poets, as you say they are, shall live at all, must they not live in their Verses, which are better, let us hope, than their bones."

Another Harvard (1828) man of letters, George S. Hillard, was unfavorably impressed during his 1847 visit. To him Shelley's was "the most interesting monument," while the epitaph of "poor Keats" was "not in good taste, though striking and characteristic; for it is a vehement expression of wounded sensibility, unsuited to a tombstone."[78]

IV

M R. WILLIAM CHARVAT, in *The Origins of American Critical Thought 1810–1835*,[1] remarks that "Keats and Shelley were neglected" and that "Keats received hardly so much as mention in the period." Just so Mr. Odell Shepard[2] says that around 1830–1834 Keats was "hardly so much" as a name "to most book-minded Americans." These statements, as the preceding sections have shown, cannot be accepted literally. It may, or may not, be true that little valuable criticism was written of Keats before 1835; but the number of books, articles, and poems in which he is featured or referred to is—unless a comparison be made to Byron —impressive. After 1830 they steadily increased, as a rapid survey will show.

A. A. Locke, editor of the *Amateur. A Cabinet of Science, Literature, and the Fine Arts*, New York and Boston, contributed to the October, 1831, issue[3] a sympathetic "literary portrait," discussing Keats in the same breath with Swift, Miss Edgeworth, and Bernard Barton. "The poems of Keats," he declared, "are full of extravagance and irregularity, rash attempts at originality, interminable wanderings, and excessive obscu-

56

rity," but "they are flushed all over with the rich lights of fancy, and so coloured and bestrewn with the flowers of poetry, that even while perplexed and bewildered in their labyrinths, it is impossible to resist the intoxication of their sweetness, or to shut our hearts to the enchantments they so lavishly present." Keats has "many lapses and failures," much "matter for ridicule," but one who does not admire and delight in his verse cannot "find any great pleasure in some of the finest creations of Milton and Shakespeare."

Then in the *American Quarterly Review*, Philadelphia, March, 1832,[4] Keats made an unexpected appearance as a "Lake Poet." Writing a review of "American Lake Poetry," Dr. James McHenry showed himself as much opposed to contemporary verse styles and to Wordsworthian critical theories as Francis Jeffrey, and attacked as imitative "Lakers" Willis, W. C. Bryant, and J. G. Percival. McHenry accused the three of using "a false style" modeled on that of the English Lakers—Wordsworth, Southey, Coleridge, Keats, Shelley, "and the whole tribe of the self-styled *'intellectual poets,'* " none of whom, after "nearly thirty years" of puffing, are "in reality popular." The Americans have "that abstruse dulness which is characteristic of the Lake poetry," just as even Byron sometimes has *"Lakish* cloudiness." Bryant "generally uses the prosaic diction of the Lake School," but, happily, "seldom indulges in the conceits and occult meanings so prevalent in the poetry of that school, particularly as it is

written by Shelley, Keats, Willis, and Percival." The
Lake Poets never can be popular: "They feel it, they
complain of it. They rail against the public for want of
taste."[5]

Such criticism was altogether unpalatable to Percival, who in 1828 had described Willis as "Wordsworth
and Mrs. Hemans lackadaisified" and Bryant, Willis,
and others as "but one hand, varying as any hand
might, even on a single sheet."[6] But McHenry was
not unique in his opposition to the English Lakers. As
Mr. R. E. Spiller[7] observes, Willis himself, Washington Irving, J. F. Cooper, and others "sought out and
praised Campbell, Montgomery, and Rogers rather
than Byron, Hazlitt, or Keats."[8] For that matter, the
Albion, New York, March 14, 1840,[9] remarked: some
readers "make what they call imagination (but which
is really fancy) the test of the poet. With them, mere
visionary creations of the brain constitute poetry. And,
in combination with . . . [quality in verse, sonorous-
ness, and imagery,] it undoubtedly does; but not of
the highest kind, unless we prefer Spenser to Shakespeare, or Keats to Pope." More significantly still, the
Southern Quarterly Review, Charleston, July, 1848,[10]
after quoting lavishly from Poe's "Raven," inquired of
its readers, "Shades of Pope and Addison, is this English poetry?"

In the periodicals Keats continued to be mentioned
with fair regularity, as in Albert G. Greene's Providence *Literary Journal*, May 31, 1834,[11] which repro-

duced from Allan Cunningham's *Biographical and Critical History of the British Literature of the Last Fifty Years* (Paris, 1834) a sketch of Shelley, Byron, and various others. The section on Keats describes *Endymion* as "a singular poem," *Hyperion* and the rest as "less mystical; but they have all more or less of the obscure and the dark" except for "a remarkably fine fragment," "The Eve of St. Agnes," of which a completely unrecognizable summary is given. Apparently Cunningham had never read "St. Agnes."

Down in Richmond, Virginia, the *Southern Literary Messenger*, April, 1836,[12] cited in a foot-note "as examples of entire poems of the purest ideality" "The Ancient Mariner," "Christabel," "Kubla Khan," "and most especially the *Sensitive Plant* of Shelley, and the *Nightingale* of Keats." But the magazines gave more attention to Wordsworth and Coleridge, Shelley, Scott, Byron, and even Croly and Campbell.[13] Indeed, the *American Quarterly Review*, June, 1836,[14] began an essay on Shelley by saying, "The three greatest poets of this century are, we think, Shelley, Wordsworth and Byron"—in that order. It barely mentioned Keats in connection with "Adonais."

As in England, many references to Keats were written to slur Tennyson. The latter had, as everybody knows, been greatly ridiculed, especially after the publication of the *Poems* of 1833. Americans who did not read J. W. Croker's tirade in the *Quarterly Review*, April, 1833,[15] had an opportunity to see it in Norton and Folsom's *Select Journal of Foreign Periodical Literature*, Boston, July, 1833.[16] It begins with the well-known sarcastic comments, all inapplicable to America, on the pretended popularity of *Endymion:*

> We certainly did not discover in that poem the same degree of merit that its more clear-sighted and prophetic admirers did. We did not foresee the unbounded popularity which has carried it through we know not how many editions; which has placed it on every table; and, what is still more unequivocal, familiarized it in every mouth. All this splendor of fame, however, though we had not the sagacity to anticipate, we have the candor to acknowledge; and we request that the publisher of the new and beautiful edition of Keats's works now in the press, with graphic illustrations of Calcott and Turner, will do us the favor and the justice to notice our conversion in his prolegomena.

New admirers of Tennyson, in reading these words, must automatically have become interested in the dead poet who, Croker insisted, inspired the faulty new poems. Later on, they could applaud the comment of the *Knickerbocker*, New York, June, 1845:[17] Croker's 1833 review is "exactly the same sort of stuff that 'killed poor KEATS;' but ALFRED was not to be knocked over so easily."

J. S. Dwight, a member of Osgood's Harvard College and Divinity School coterie and later of the Transcendental Club and the Brook Farm colony, is credited by Lounsbury[18] with publishing[19] the first American criticism of Tennyson's 1830 and 1833 poems. Like countless others, he perceived the analogy between the reviewers' treatment of Keats and of his young disciple:

The Quarterly took occasion to sing over our author the *palinode* of that deadly song, in which it had before triumphed over the unfortunate Keats. It had thought to have laid forever the shade of Keats some dozen years ago; but now must needs make war upon this new-risen modest bard, in whom it shrewdly affects to discover some lineaments of its old enemy.[20]

American journals prove that the denunciations of the *Quarterly* were unavailing. Not infrequently they quote lines from Keats as casually as from Shakespeare, as when the *New-York Review*, January, 1838,[21] cites "the words of poor Keats, 'tower in the van Of all the congregated world,' "[22] and the *United States Magazine and Democratic Review*, Washington, January, June, 1839,[23] prints a poem with the quoted title, "A Thing of Beauty Is a Joy Forever," and another with the same subtitle.[24] Amusingly enough, one Clio tried to palm off verses of Keats as her (or his) own to the *New York Literary Gazette*. The editor tartly notified Clio that "the original part of . . . [his] communication is not good, and the good part is not original. We copy the following lines [85–95 of "Sleep and Poetry"] for their great beauty, knowing, however, that they are borrowed—from Keats, we believe."[25]

In the Middle West, according to Mr. Rusk,[26] Wordsworth, Coleridge, Shelley, and Keats "were little noticed in the midst of the excitement attending the triumphal reception of Byron and Scott"; "in libraries and sales collections during the period ending in 1840, there is only scant testimony" of their "fame." The case was entirely different in the East, where well-read Americans knew Keats and his four satellite poets, Coleridge, Shelley, Mrs. Howitt, and Milman, about as well as they knew Bryant, Lowell, Holmes, and Longfellow. Van Wyck Brooks[27] patronizingly refers to "a 'band' of aesthetic youths and maidens" who around 1840 "gathered in Cambridge and Watertown," Massachusetts, to read "Keats and Tennyson together." As Keats still is and Tennyson then was the poet of youth, very likely such bands, esthetic or not, assembled elsewhere.

There were, of course, a few dissenters among important men of letters. Possibly Bronson Alcott should be included among them. According to Mr. Odell Shepard,[28] during his stay (1830–1834) in Germantown, Pennsylvania, Alcott read Coleridge, Wordsworth, Shelley, Byron, "and even Keats," but "Keats remained to him hardly more than a name." On the contrary, Miss Dorothy McCuskey[29] asserts that "he particularly enjoyed the English romantic poets, Wordsworth, Coleridge, Byron, Shelley, and Keats, who, with Milton, he considered the 'first poets in the language.'" Emerson was decidedly hostile to both Keats and Shelley, as his journals prove. "There is," says Mr. Rusk,[30] "not much about either of them until 1840," and as late as 1868 Emerson had "only mild enthusiasm for

Keats," saying, "Keats *had* poetic genius, though I could well spare the whole Endymion." In the *Dial*, October, 1840,[31] Emerson had paid his disrespects to one of the Philadelphia versions of Galignani. Speaking of "the Feeling of the Infinite," he declared:

Nothing certifies the prevalence of this taste in the people more than the circulation of the poems,—one would say, most incongruously united by some bookseller,—of Coleridge, Shelley, and Keats. The only unity is in the subjectiveness and the aspiration common to the three writers.[32] Shelley . . . is never a poet.

Hawthorne, on the contrary, read Keats with pleasure. In one of his most charming sketches (about 1842), "P.'s Correspondence,"[33] P. writes from England on February 29, 1845, of the various literary figures whom he has supposedly seen and chatted with. P. "can hardly think . . . [Keats] a great poet," yet those who have seen his epic think it the "loftiest" poetry since Milton. He promises, if he obtains specimens, to send them to Hawthorne for Lowell, "who seems to be one of the poet's most fervent and worthiest worshippers."

Mr. T. O. Mabbott[34] has already called attention to the New York magazine *Arcturus*, which in December, 1841,[35] printed an essay on a comparatively new theme, "The Sonnets of Keats." "The world," it asserts, "has now definitely settled the point for its own satisfaction that Keats was a poet. We can only wonder that it should have ever been doubted by any one." Keats "wrote like Milton in his minor poems," but prejudice

63

against his associates ruined his reputation. "With true humility and love should we approach an author like Keats." "A small but sacred shelf in the library may hold the few brothers in time who have thus far thought and felt with his youthful exuberance"—some Greeks, Shakespeare, Sidney, and the youthful Milton. Sonnets by the three English poets are then quoted, and Keats' "On Chapman's Homer" is described as the "noblest." "When we think of Keats, tenderly and sadly, for his early death and wounded spirit," the essay goes on, "there should be triumph too, in this immortal mind, which can prevail over gloom and disaster, and write its story in imperishable song." In January, 1842,[36] *Arcturus* printed a sonnet by Lowell "To the Spirit of Keats" ("Great soul, thou sittest with me in my room") and reprinted from Hunt's *Indicator*[37] "La Belle Dame sans Merci." The editors profess themselves "glad to find, by the voices and rejoicings of the press," that "we did not in our last [number] sing too loudly" Keats' praise; "we say welcome to the enthusiasm of the newspapers."[38] But somewhat earlier the *Albion*, New York, November 20, 1841,[39] had published the following unsigned poem:

KEATS.

The world he dwelt in was a solitude;
> And he a flitting shade,—a spectre pale,—
> A voice, like that embodied in the gale,
When in its softest whisper it hath wooed
A Naiad in her cave. Earth's common brood,

Trampling the flowers, which Heaven's own
   sweets exhale
Looked on him as a glow-worm, or a snail,
Crushed under foot, if in their way it stood:
And so they crushed him.
             'Twas a grateful boon,
  To send him early from this world of sorrows;
For his young heart, dried up and withered soon,
  Having no joy, save what from love it borrows—
Love, like his own Endymion's for the moon—
  And hope, the rainbow spanning our to-morrows.

In the *Southern Literary Messenger*, January, 1842,[40] Tuckerman returned to his old love with an article on "Keats,"[41] defending the poet against aspersions of unmanliness, and insisting that no reviewer killed him. Once more he told of visiting Keats' grave—though, still following Hunt, he gave the date of the poet's death as December 27, 1820.[42] Tuckerman was especially enamored of "The Eve of St. Agnes," which "for invention, structure, imagery, and all the elements of the art, is as faultless and as rare a gem as can be found in English literature. . . . If it does not live, it will be because taste and the love of the beautiful have died." But in spite of Tuckerman's eulogy, the *Southern Literary Messenger* gave comparatively little attention to Keats, apart from incidental references, as in June, 1840, April, 1841, and September, 1842.[43] The issue for April, 1844,[44] indeed, has a savage criticism of "Tennyson's Poems," in the course of which Tennyson is reproached for having "adopted Keats' style of rhyming, bringing in ideas for the sake of the rhyme, and contenting himself with a faint jingle of sound."

In sharp contrast is the article, "St. Agnes' Eve. A Chit-Chat about Keats," with the familiar signature of "Jeremy Short," in *Graham's Magazine*, Philadelphia, April, 1842.[45] "I have shed tears over his grave at Rome —let us drink to his memory in solemn silence," it begins, before indulging in superlatives.

Everything he wrote evinced high genius. Each successive poem he published displayed increased merit. His sonnets remind me of Milton—his shorter pieces breathe of Lycidas or Venus and Adonis. . . . Few men had a finer perception of the beautiful. . . . He is one of the most Grecian . . . of our poets.

The "Grecian Urn" is "delicious." But "St. Agnes" is the poem for which Keats will be loved. . . . It is as superior to Endymion as a star to a satellite. . . . It has the glow of a landscape seen through a rosy glass—it is warm and blushing, yet pure as a maiden in her first exceeding beauty. . . . What luxuriance of fancy, what scope of language, what graphic power it displays! It is a love story, and right witchingly told. How exquisite the description of Madeline, her moonlit chamber, her awakening from her dream, and the delicious intoxicating emotions which break on her when she learns that she loves and is beloved.

The story is then retold by summary and lavish quotations. "St. Agnes" shows that Keats was "a genius," but *Hyperion* "evinces . . . even more of the '*mens divinior*.'" "With many faults, it evinces more genius than any poem since written in our language." "We will never forgive the Quarterly for having disheartened Keats from the completion of this poem."

Graham's was edited for a time by Rufus W. Griswold. His biographer, Joy Bayless,[46] narrates how in 1830, aged fifteen, he ran away to Albany, New York, to live with George G. Foster, later a popular yellow journalist, who "led him into a new world of books," and how "the romantic poets—Shelley, Keats, Wordsworth, and the beloved Byron—were read by the two friends at night in the room which they shared," with Griswold preferring the neoclassicists, Foster the romantics. Such preferences Griswold never entirely lost, and in the September, 1842, issue of *Graham's*[47] he tartly objected to "a critic for whose judgment we have great respect," who had called Tennyson "the first original English poet since Keats." Various American poets, he asserted, have plagiarized from "him who 'stole at first hand from Keats,' " but, in any case, "Bryant, Longfellow, and others" are superior to Keats' plagiarist.[48]

Meanwhile, to the first number, January, 1842, of Nathan Hale, Jr.'s *Boston Miscellany of Literature and Fashion*[49] Lowell, a Harvard classmate of Hale's, had contributed a "Sonnet.—To Keats" ("Thine eyes, I know, with earnestness were fraught"). In the October issue[50] the Columbia graduate William A. Jones published an essay on "Later Sonnets," wherein he remarked:

Wordsworth, Coleridge [!], and Keats are the writers of

the genuine sonnet, in this nineteenth century, and by far the best poets. The majestic tone and deep feeling of the first, the learned invention and universality of talent of the second, and the exuberant fancy of the third, can fitly be measured by none but the same standards that we apply to the old Elizabethan poets and to Milton. . . . A late article in Arcturus Magazine (Dec. 1841,) has done him [Keats] true poetic justice. To this delicate appreciation . . . we can add nothing, but only contribute a hearty assent. The hour has come at last for Keats, that always comes to the true poet. A brother bard, (J. R. Lowell,) whose first volume contains passages and poems Keats would have been willing to acknowledge, and whose own delicate genius enables him to appreciate a cognate talent, has done honor to the English bard in stanzas, that put to the blush all prose criticisms.

To the same magazine, then called the *Boston Miscellany and Lady's Monthly Magazine* and edited by Tuckerman, in January, 1843,[51] George Lunt, Harvard class of 1824, contributed "The Nightingale,"[52] which imitates Keats perhaps too closely. It ends thus:

> Oh! for a draught of vintage such as this,
> > To meet my kiss!
> Filled to the blushing brim with dreams of old,
> > And bubbling gold!
> Those sad deep minstrelsies, oh, Nightingale,
> > Like thy lorn wail;
> That fill the minstrel-heart, 'till raptures make
> > The heartstrings break,
> Breathing life out in the sad melody
> > Of a sweet sigh!

Early in 1841 J. F. Clarke returned from the west to Boston, where he founded a new Unitarian Church of the Disciples. The April, 1843, number of Emerson's transcendental magazine, the Boston *Dial*,[53] included his well-known article, an unqualified eulogy of George Keats, who "not only loved his brother John, but reverenced his genius, and enjoyed his poetry, believing him to belong to the front rank of English bards. Modern criticism seems disposed to concur with this judgment." Clarke appended verses written by "this great author," as well as "Remarks on John Milton, By John Keats, Written in the Flyleaf of Paradise Lost."[54]

Emerson's friend and former editor, Margaret Fuller, thought differently. She had eulogized the work of Shelley in the *Boston Quarterly Review,* July, 1840,[55] and in the *Dial* itself, April, 1841,[56] had published a long article about him by John M. Mackie, an 1832 graduate of Brown University.[57] Though by August, 1842, she "loved" Tennyson and had "taken him to heart as a brother,"[58] his master Keats was another matter. It is difficult to acquit Miss Fuller of personal prejudice against the American Keatses, with whom, through Clarke and her own sister Ellen (later wife of the poet W. E. Channing), she was intimately connected. Margaret had occasionally corresponded in lofty tone with George Keats,[59] in whose house the school-teacher Ellen lived for a time; but the latter's misconduct towards Emma Keats Speed, graphically described in a letter George sent to Clarke on July 4,

1841, brought the Fuller-Keats friendships to an end.[60] Perhaps for this reason, when Miss Fuller composed a long article on "Modern British Poets,"[61] she began by saying: "Nine muses were enough for one Greece, and nine poets are enough for one country, even in the nineteenth century. And these nine are a 'sacred nine,' who, if not quite equal to Shakspeare, Spenser, and Milton, are fairly initiated masters of the wand and spell." The "sacred nine" turn out to be Campbell, Moore, Scott, Crabbe, Shelley, Byron, Southey, Coleridge, and Wordsworth. Keats is not even mentioned, and the omission does no credit to the author's critical powers. Mrs. Sarah Whitman, of Providence, aptly characterized them in a letter (1846?) to Miss Ida Russell: "I have known her more than once to mistake a nightingale for a magpie—Witness her judgment and condemnation of poor Keats—a sentence which in compliance with the highest authorities she would now doubtless, gladly reverse."[62]

Sargent's New Monthly Magazine, New York, May, 1843,[63] contains a violent attack by "P." on "Blackwood and Its Editor," John Wilson. It flatly declares that "the lack of all honesty . . . which characterizes what are called Wilson's 'scorching,' and 'withering' notices of Hunt, Hazlitt, Keats, and Barry Cornwall, is utterly indefensible on any principles," and tells how to Wilson, or "Christopher North," "the author of St. Agnes Eve and Hyperion, little 'Johnnie Keats,' is a puling young cockney, whose impertinence in printing his babyish twattle is deserving of the most stinging rebuke." A contributor to the June issue,[64] however, ridiculed "literary goslings" who abstract "a little nonsense from Keats, and more from Tennison [*sic*]; some pantheism from Shelley," and so on; while the editor, Epes Sargent, himself omitted Keats from his *Selections in Poetry for Exercises at School and at Home*, Philadelphia, 1853.

Likewise Mrs. Anna C. Lowell, in her *Poetry for Home and School*, Boston, 1843, included selections from practically all the important modern poets except Keats, and failed to rectify the omission in later editions, as in 1846 and 1851.[65] But that poet received his due in the New York edition of R. H. Horne's *A New Spirit of the Age*, 1844. Writing about Tennyson,[66] Horne quotes the London *Times*, December 26, 1842, as saying that Keats has "had the greatest influence on that which is now the popular poetry," that to young poets Keats is immortal. Horne praises Keats at length. "There is no poet," he declares, "ancient or modern, upon whom the title of 'Divine' can be more appropriately conferred than upon Keats."[67] Horne discusses his influence on Tennyson, and elsewhere in the volume[68] makes incidental laudatory references to him.

Willis, who had done so much to build Keats' early reputation, continued that good work in the various editions of *Pencillings by the Way* and elsewhere. Then in February, 1844, he and G. P. Morris, editors of the

71

New Mirror, New York, compiled the *Mirror Library*, the sale of which was probably considerable, since the editors had numerous agents not only in New York and elsewhere in the East but as far west as Michigan and Illinois and as far south as Alabama and Louisiana. Part 8 of the *Mirror Library*, entitled "The Rococo, No. 1," contains "three of the most delicious Poems ever written," Drake's "Culprit Fay," W. M. Praed's "Lillian," and Keats' "St. Agnes." The text of the last and the elaborate commentary that accompanies it are reprinted without acknowledgment from *Leigh Hunt's London Journal*, January 21, 1835.[69] In his concluding "Notes" Willis makes the unhappy remark that the poems are "the three most exquisite and absolute creations of pure imagination . . . that have been produced since Shakspere," and the far happier assertion: "It almost requires a poet to appreciate the unreachable delicacy of Keats's use of language. He plucks his epithets from the profoundest hiding-places of meaning and association."

Up to 1844, however, Campbell attracted more attention than Keats,[70] and among the numerous articles lamenting his death (June 15) and praising his literary achievement that reprinted from John Dix deserves mention. In the *Albion*, August 24, 1844,[71] Dix describes a talk he had with Campbell in London during 1838. Their subject was the English poets, and it is edifying to read Campbell's judgments. "Keats' poems, he said, were too laboured. The 'Ode to a Nightingale,' he considered his best production," while Shelley is "a poet for poets only." To another visitor, "A Cosmopolitan,"[72] Campbell had been more expansive. The Nightingale Ode, he said,

is unquestionably the finest thing Keats ever did—and he had more of the pure spirit of poetry in him, Shelley alone excepted, perhaps, than any other writer of modern days. What a pity that he should have been so thin skinned. Hunt, and the rest of that squad, did him no good, by nursing his conceits, but had he lived he would have taken his own ground—and kept it.

Rufus W. Griswold was judicious and favorable. In the preface to his Philadelphia anthology, *The Poets and Poetry of England, in the Nineteenth Century,* 1845,[73] he spoke of "the classic imagery" of Keats. Eleven pages (301–311)[74] are devoted to the poems, but Griswold's memoir adds nothing whatever: indeed, it goes back to Hunt's biography, and hence gives an incorrect date for the poet's death. In its conclusion readers are assured:

KEATS was the greatest of all poets who have died so young. His imagination, which he most delighted to indulge through the medium of mythological fable, was affluent and warm. Some of his pictures of this kind are rich beyond any similar productions in our language. They have a voluptuous glow, that prove a keen and passionate sense of the beautiful. The loose versification of many of his works has induced belief that he lacked energy proportionate to the vividness of his conceptions; but the opinion is wrong. Many of his sonnets possess a Miltonic vigour, and his "Eve of St. Agnes," is as highly finished, almost, as the masterpieces of POPE.

Griswold, of course, attracted considerable attention from the press. Reviewing him, E. P. Whipple[75] said of Keats: "Since his death, it has become a common cant to speak of him as possessing something Miltonic in his genius." Reviews killed him "because he was weak." Keats is "a kind of youthful Spenser, without Spenser's moral sense or judgment." He is "faint and languid." "The Eve of St. Agnes" "is delicately beautiful, and perfect of its kind; but it is not poetry of the highest order," "it has no grand imaginations." Whipple thought[76] that Jeffrey "appears to considerable advantage" in his 1820 *Edinburgh Review* criticism of Keats. As for William Gifford,[77] to him "for a time belonged the equivocal fame of killing John Keats; but we are glad that a disclosure of the facts has lately robbed him of this laurel of slander. It is quite a satisfaction to know, that even the tenderest and most sensitive of poets was beyond the reach of his envenomed arrows."

On the whole, Whipple's is a hostile criticism. No hostility appears in the comments of his contemporary G. W. Curtis, and no American has ever surpassed him in love for Keats' verse. To Dwight, once his fellow-resident at Brook Farm, he wrote on June 28, 1844,[78] "Shelley and Keats are associated always together in my mind," and then he composed impromptu quatrains on each. "But," he added, "you must write your

74

own poem upon them before you will be satisfied."
To the same correspondent on March 13, 1845,[79] he
said: "Milton fused in Keats would have formed a
greater than Shakespeare." In his letters to the poetess,
Sarah Whitman,[80] Curtis was more rhapsodic still.
Thus, writing from Concord, April 9, 1845:[81] "With
Shelley . . . Poetry was an elegant and passionate pur-
suit. He was too much a Scholar. . . . With Keats,
Poetry was an intense life. It was a vital, golden fire,
that burned him up." Mrs. Whitman replied so en-
thusiastically as to evoke the following comments on
June 2:

I am glad that you speak so truly of Keats. It is rare to find
any one who has the just appreciation of his genius. It is
of that nature which is too much condemned, or too much
praised. . . . There lay in him the keenest and most delicate
perception and the truest feeling. Tho't was all fused with
sentiment. Poetry was to him an element such as music would
be to some natures. His blood seemed to thrill, rather than
flow thro' his veins, and I always picture him as in ecstasy.[82]

Caroline Ticknor[83] observes: "Throughout his correspondence Curtis dwells much upon his intense ad-
miration for Keats and Shelley, in regard to whose
work he carries on long discussions with Mrs. Whitman, urging her to write an essay upon Keats, to match
one which she had written on Shelley." A final specimen may be cited from Curtis' letter dated February
6, 1846:[84] There was a "spiritual voluptuousness"
in Keats, as in Shelley, but in the former it was "more

fiery and intense. It sucked up his whole being at times, so that its expression syllabled fire and passion, as in the invocation to the moon in *Endymion*. In Shelley it was less ardent and never of that fierce lavishness which it was in Keats." To Mrs. Cranch on February 25, 1849,[85] Curtis wrote: "Keats died a boy. He was tangled in his own magnificent luxuriance. How I do love these men, Keats, Shelley, Tennyson, and Browning."

All along, English criticisms were being reprinted in America, and some of them had considerable impact. Leigh Hunt was especially popular, and when his *Imagination and Fancy* appeared at New York in 1845 it attracted much attention. A number of reviewers mentioned his criticism of Keats, to which were appended poems with explanatory and critical notes.[86] On the famous line from "St. Agnes," "As though a rose should shut, and be a bud again," Hunt asks, "Can the beautiful go beyond this? I never saw it."[87] More eulogistic still is the long essay on "the hapless apothecary's boy" in George Gilfillan's *Sketches of Modern Literature, and Eminent Literary Men*[88] (New York and Philadelphia, 1846). Gilfillan said: " 'Hyperion' is the greatest of poetical Torsos"; "The Eve of St. Agnes" is "a dream within a dream. Its every line wears *couleur de rose*"; "in originality Keats has seldom been surpassed. His works 'rise like an exhalation.' " "His genius lay in his body like sun-fire in a dew-drop, at once beautifying and burning it up." Of an entirely different nature is the entertaining anecdote in Walter C. Dendy's *The Philosophy of Mystery* (London, 1841), which was reprinted at New York in 1845 and 1847. Dendy tells[89] of

the romantic poet of Endymion, who . . . gave up the study of that science which might have nursed and fortified a mind so soon chilled to death by the icy fingers of criticism. Erato was the mistress of John Keats; but while he wooed, he perished. . . . Even in the lecture-room of Saint Thomas's I have seen Keats in a deep poetic dream: his mind was on Parnassus with the Muses.

Dendy gives "a quaint [prose] fragment which he one evening scribbled in our presence, while the precepts of Sir Astley Cooper fell unheeded on his ear."

A reviewer of Gilfillan in the *United States Magazine, and Democratic Review*, New York, January, 1846,[90] thinking of philosophers, scientists, and historians, strongly objected to his calling Wordsworth, Southey, and Keats "the *leading stars* in the bright host of our literary heaven," since *belles lettres* do not "constitute the highest walk of intellect." "It implies utter confusion of mind . . . to propose a standard of greatness which shall make of Lamb or Keats the *decora et tutamina* of the modern world." Dwight, however, cordially reviewed the *Sketches* in the *Harbinger* of Brook Farm, January 10, 1846.[91] In that journal of transcendentalism, to which Curtis and Cranch were also contributors, Clarke, on March 21, 1846,[92] briefly noticed the Wiley and Putnam edition of Keats' *Poems*, looked forward "to a still greater treat in Milne's [*sic*] edition," and reprinted from the 1836 *Western Messenger* the "Apollo" ode. Again, Dwight, on May 16,[93] discussed the verse of Thomas Hood, whom he recognized as "one of the most classic, original, imaginative and deeply inspired bards of modern England, one to be named with Tennyson and Keats." His *Hero and Leander* "has a Grecian warmth and quaint delicacy of imagination, worthy of the best mythologic dreams of Keats."[94]

References to Keats now became increasingly common and laudatory, many of them being tied up with criticism of Tennyson. *Graham's Magazine*, January, 1847,[95] for example, took issue with Bulwer-Lytton for a passage in *The New Timon* (1846), where he "most ignorantly and pertly ridicules" Keats, Tennyson, and Wordsworth. The *Southern Literary Messenger*, February, 1847,[96] left that ridicule unreproved, but included the first and last poets in "a constellation of bright stars" which "gladdened the world's eye—Byron, Shelley, Keats, Wordsworth, Moore, and fifty others, 'Worthy on Fame's eternal bead-rod [*sic*] to be filed.' " But Lowell, in the *North American Review*, April, 1847,[97] wrote of Bulwer: "His allusions to Wordsworth, Tennyson, and Keats are presumptuous and in bad taste. The fact that he misspells the name of one of these poets [Keates] argues either a very petty affectation, or a shameful unfamiliarity with what he pretends to criticize."

During 1847, indeed, it was scarcely possible for readers to avoid running across the name and verse of Keats. In February, to illustrate, *Graham's Magazine*[98] gave the text of two sonnets by Hunt "On Receiving a Crown of Ivy from John Keats" ("A crown of ivy! I submit my head," "It is a lofty feeling, yet a kind") from manuscript copies in Keats' *Poems*, 1817, that George Keats had given to Fortunatus Cosby, Jr., of Louisville. Also in Louisville Ben Casseday, compiling *The Poetic Lacon* (New York and Philadelphia), included various extracts from Keats.[99] Then the *Homes and Haunts of the Most Eminent British Poets* by William Howitt, a Keats-worshiper for thirty years, was published at New York by Harper. Though Howitt based his biographical sketch entirely on Hunt, his own comments on Keats approach hyperbole: as that he "was one of those sweet and glorious spirits who descend, like the angel messengers of old, to discharge some divine command, not to dwell here"; "his nature was one pure mass of the living light of poetry"; "there is no poet, living or dead, except Shakespeare, who can pretend to any thing like the felicity of epithet which characterizes Keats"; "the most magnificent trophy of his genius . . . is the fragment of Hyperion."[100] Howitt's book was widely read—it was favorably reviewed in *Graham's Magazine* for August[101]—and a new edition was soon called for.

Mere reiteration made an impact even on critics of a more or less neoclassical bent. "We confess we have no great love for modern poetry . . . ," writes one of them in the *United States Magazine, and Democratic Review,* November, 1847;[102] "we prefer the poetry of past ages." Yet the unhappy life and death of Keats have aroused his sympathy. That poet "forced himself into notice . . . by the modest, winning beauties of his muse. His spirit seemed too etherial for earth." But he would live forever "if the sole evidence" of his "poetical inspiration had been his 'Eve of Saint Agnes.' " Posterity will know him "by isolated and individual beauties of verse," for "his poetry has all the extravagancies and errors of youth," "his sense of beauty" is "a disease." "He painted every thing *couleur de rose.* His rich and prolific fancy transformed all surrounding objects into gold." All literary history shows no instance of "more gross and manifest injustice, than the atrocious and savage assault upon Keats by the Quarterly Review." The writer then takes Gifford, the supposed assaulter, to task, and tells of his alleged effect on the poet. "He pined, sickened, and died. He had given bright promise of superior poetical powers, but withered before his prime."

In January, 1848, the *Knickerbocker,*[103] without any comment at all, reprinted the Englishman W. C. Bennett's "Sonnet: To Keats" ("Oh nightingale, thou wert for golden Junes"),[104] thereby partially atoning for its rather striking neglect of the poet. The *Albion,* February 12,[105] did better with a (reprinted?) article on "The Poetry of Diet," in which emphasis is given to

"St. Agnes," "a beautiful poem by that wonderful young poet Keats," "one of the most beautiful poems in the English language," a "poetic gem." After summarizing the story and quoting the lovely description of the midnight banquet dishes, the author exclaims: "How much of united delicacy and richness is here! There is no overloading, no gaudy ornament—all is chaste and refined, but at the same time exquisitely rich and luxurious. It is a collation worthy of Elysium, to be partaken of by Apollo and the Muses." Again on May 20[106] it reprinted an essay on "Coleridge and Keats," in which J. W. Lester rhapsodized: Keats "was nature itself—as divine, as rich, as delicious"; "the boy had a gigantic soul; it was endowed with grandeur and tremendous power." After all these verbal bouquets it seems too bad that the philosopher Francis Bowen, a Harvard contemporary (1830–1833) of Clarke and Osgood, should have chastised Keats, Byron, Coleridge, Shelley, and Wordsworth by saying:[107] "Each . . . has apparently been quite as anxious to make the public acquainted with himself as with his works; they have all displayed, though in a greater or less degree, both egotism and spleen."

V

OPINIONS MAY differ about the value of the early criticism of Keats, but by 1848 it had established him in the American mind as a great poet. In regard to America's own poets the *Athenaeum*, 1835,[1] declared, "Wordsworth and Mrs. Hemans are their models, rather than Byron. Mrs. Hemans has, perhaps, exercised a more visible influence upon the poetry of America than any other writer."[2] A contemporary authority, Mr. William Charvat,[3] insists that "in the American romantic period up to 1860, there was little of the influence of Shelley and Keats in the mature work of our best poets." Influence, a delicate and vexed subject on which generalizations are hard to check, is outside the province of this sketch. The influence of Keats certainly was much less than that of Byron, Wordsworth, Coleridge, and Campbell, but whether or not American poets before 1848 show Keatsian influence, nearly all had read him. Nearly all, too, praised him. J. G. Whittier did so by implication in 1832: "What poet of modern days has ever published a perfect volume?" Not Byron, Southey, Wordsworth, Shelley; not Keats, for "the author of St. Agnes Eve is mawkish and affected in his Endymion."[4]

Among poets who read, praised, and sometimes imitated Keats, Drake, Halleck, Pike, Cranch, Lunt, Bryant, Fairfield, Morris, Percival, Willis, Mrs. Whitman, Lowell, Taylor, and others have already been mentioned. Hence only a few additional details need be given.

Halleck included the odes on "The Nightingale," "The Grecian Urn," and "Psyche" in his *Selections from the British Poets* (New York, 1840).[5] He must have been pleased to read in 1848[6] that he himself "for twenty years *at least,* has been permitted to hold an honourable place in the illustrious catalogue" of nineteenth-century poets with "Byron, Shelley, Southy [*sic*], Moore, Campbell, Burns, Bloomfield, Coleridge, Tennyson, Keats."

Students of Poe have found Keatsian influence in poems as early as the "Sonnet—To Science" (1829) and "The Sleeper" (1831).[7] Apparently Poe got a copy of the Galignani Coleridge-Shelley-Keats late in 1830 or early in 1831, and of it many traces have been detected in his subsequent verses. His earliest references to Keats are, in general, unilluminating. In 1837 he refused to assign Bryant "a place with the spiritual Shelleys, or Coleridges, or Wordsworths, or with Keats, or even Tennyson, or Wilson, or with some other burning lights of our own day, to be valued in a day to come";[8] in March, 1842,[9] he ranked Keats in the company of Shelley, Coleridge, and Tennyson. Then in a letter to Lowell, July 2, 1844,[10] he confessed: "I am profoundly excited . . . by some poems,—those of Tennyson especially,—whom, with Keats, Shelley, Coleridge (occasionally), and a few others of like thought and expression, I regard as the *sole* poets." In a conversation with Chivers at New York in the summer of 1845, Poe was asked the question, "What do you think of Keats?"

"He was the greatest of any of the English Poets of the same age, if not at any age," answered he, with the air of a man who was not only conscious of his own consummate ability, but who had, long before, deliberately formed his opinions. "He was far in advance of the best of them, with the exception of Shelley, in the study of his themes. His principal fault is the grotesqueness of his abandon."[11]

Chivers himself in 1837 visited Philadelphia, where he read one of the Coleridge-Shelley-Keats editions with care. S. F. Damon[12] says that this year "marks the influence of these poets (Keats in particular) on Chivers," and he gives abundant details. When Chivers returned to his home at Oaky Grove, Georgia,[13] he rewrote (May 10) "The Dying Poet,"[14] with the prefixed quotation, " 'I feel the daisies growing over me!' *Keats' Dying Words*," the fifth and last stanza of which runs:

> I see that earth cannot suffice
>> To give my spirit rest;
> I now must go above the skies,
>> And sing among the blest.

Lowell was so devoted to Keats that in 1840 he planned to become his biographer, and went "so far as to write a letter to his brother George—which I never sent."[15] It is a pity that he gave up the plan, for he could have obtained material from George Keats to supplement that available at a later date to Milnes. Lowell's own indebtedness to Keats was commented on by practically all his reviewers. According to *Graham's Magazine*, April, 1842, he could "emulate the ideality of Tennyson and Keats without the affectation of the one, or the redundancy of the other."[16] No doubt these words pleased him, for his love for both poets was deep-rooted. In *Conversations on Some of the Old Poets* (Cambridge, 1845),[17] he recorded his belief that "Keats saw deeper into the mystery of this noble metre [blank verse] than any modern poet," and that he "has written, perhaps, the best ode in the language, upon" the nightingale. Again,

Keats and Tennyson are both masters of description, but Keats had the finer ear for all the nice analogies and suggestions of sound, while his eye had an equally instinctive rectitude of perception in color. Tennyson's epithets suggest a silent picture; Keat's [*sic*] the very thing itself, with its sound or stillness. . . . If Tennyson's mind be more sensitive, Keat's is grander and of a larger grasp. . . . It will be centuries before another nature so spontaneously noble and majestic as that of Keats, and so tender and merciful, too, is embodied.[18]

Finally,

the world is not yet aware of the wonderful merit of Keats.

Men have squabbled about Chatterton, and written lives of Kirke White, while they have treated with contempt the rival, and, I will dare to say, the sometimes superior, of Milton. . . . Keats can afford to wait, and he will yet be sacred to the hearts of all those who love the triumphs and ovations of our noble mother-tongue.[19]

A reviewer in *Graham's Magazine,* March, 1845,[20] was unable to agree with these last remarks. Lowell, he contended, "informs us that Keats is the rival, and sometimes the superior of Milton. But we gladly pass over such information as this, to come to the real merits of the book."[21]

Three Boston volumes of 1847 deserve cursory mention: Longfellow's *The Estray: A Collection of Poems;* Thomas Buchanan Read's *Poems;* and W. E. Channing, the younger's, *Poems,* Second Series. In the first, an anthology of old and contemporary verse, Keats is appropriately represented by the "Ode on a Grecian Urn."[22] Read, who in smallness of stature and delicacy of features resembled Keats, wrote of "The Bards"— "The world-wide Shakspeare—the imperial Spenser," "While delicate, as from a silver censer, Float the sweet dreams of Keats!"[23] Channing concluded his volume with tactless verses "Of Keats":[24]

> 'T is said, a Keats by critics, once was killed,
> Alas! they have lacked power to do this thing
> In these late days, or else some blood was spilled,
> They softly bite to-day, or kick and fling. . . .

Of Keats' poetry I have small taste,
But trust some Critics still are in the field,
Whose well-puffed Pills are not composed of paste,
Whose swords of lath with wisdom they do wield.

For me, I trust they will not spare one line,
Or else in frozen silence may abide,
Pray may they hack like butchers at all mine,
And kill me like that Keats if it betide. . . .

The *Southern Quarterly Review*, Charleston, April, 1847,[25] leaped to the attack: "He threatens—he, the heavy, conceited egotist, to imitate that sickly and sorrowful youth Keats, whose whole nature was sensitive as a naked nerve,—and to die of a broken heart!" The writer doubted that "Mr. Channing can ever die of wounded sensibility." In the same vein, the *Southern Literary Messenger*, May, 1847,[26] declared: "The lines are founded on the old myth about Keats being killed by an article in the Quarterly. We wish another hero had been chosen, as the name of this one is rather unmanageable in verse. . . . Mr. Channing need not be alarmed; we are fully satisfied that he is not a Keats, and that the utmost malice of the critics cannot harm him." In the *Harbinger*, January 23, 1847,[27] however, Channing's fellow-Brook-Farmer, Dwight, had loyally written: "Mr. CHANNING's volume closes with a challenge to the critics, apropos to Keats' case. We like it, except his estimate of Keats."

Only a few other poets can be mentioned. The great-

est of all, Walt Whitman, wrote on March 5, 1846:
"Keats—peace to his ashes—was one of the pleasant-
est of modern poets, and, had not the grim monster
Death so early claimed him, would doubtless have become one of the most distinguished."[28] He also included Keats in the seven years of reading that preceded the composition of *Leaves of Grass* (1855), but
his reactions were, on the whole, unfavorable. In one
of his early notes Whitman said:

Keats' poetry is ornamental, elaborated, rich in wrought
imagery, it is imbued with the sentiment, at second-hand, of
the gods and goddesses of twenty-five hundred years ago.
Its feeling is the feeling of a gentlemanly person lately at
college, accepting what was commanded him there, who
moves and would only move in elegant society, reading classical books in libraries. Of life in the nineteenth century it
has none any more than the statues have. It does not come
home at all to the direct wants of the bodies and souls of the
century.[29]

Philip Pendleton Cooke, of Virginia, took the atti-
tude of Lowell, not Whitman. At Princeton University
or later, Keats, Shelley, and Coleridge (the names
point once again to the influence of the Philadelphia
volumes) became his favorites.[30] In the preface, November 10, 1846, to *Froissart Ballads, and Other Poems*
(Philadelphia, 1847), Cooke remarks that "versifica-
tions of old stories . . . were customary with the noblest poets of our English language," and, hence, "until the world thinks the less of the Canterbury Tales,

or of the Basil Pot of John Keats, for the fact that they trace to" Boccaccio, he hopes to be justified in his own plan of writing. *Graham's Magazine*, May, 1847,[31] thought no justification necessary: the book "fully deserves the hearty reception, which we are glad to see so universally extended to it by the press."

A more open imitator, William Lord, had issued his *Poems* at New York and Philadelphia in 1845. Poe gleefully demolished it.[32] *Graham's Magazine*,[33] however, was flattering enough, while making the point that Lord's

style gives repeated evidence of an unconscious indebtedness to Spenser, Keats, Shelley, Coleridge and Wordsworth, especially to the two first. . . . By the sensitiveness of his mind, he catches the melody and spirit of the poems which have strongly affected his sympathies, and naturally reproduces them. "Saint Mary's Gift"[34] is a compound of Spenser and Keats; it has just enough of the former to distinguish it from "St. Agnes' Eve," and just enough of the latter to distinguish it from the "Faery Queene."

Actually the echoes of Keats are far from "unconscious." In "Saint Mary's Gift" plot, characterization, and language were deliberately, if none too artistically, imitated; while in his "Ode to England"[35] Lord named his masters, Chaucer, Spenser, Shakespeare, and others, singling out Keats thus:

Oh gold Hyperion, love-lorn Porphyro,
Ill-fated! from thine orbed fire struck back

Just as the parting clouds began to glow,
   And stars, like sparks, to bicker in thy track! . . .
   His lips shall never taste the immortal wine,
Who sought to drain the glowing cup too soon,
For he hath perished, and the moon
Hath lost Endymion—but too well
   The shaft that pierced him in her arms was sped:—
   Into that gulf of dark and nameless dread,
   Star-like he fell, but a wide splendor shed
Through its deep night, that kindled as he fell.

This cursory sketch may end with the Philadelphia poet, Henry B. Hirst, a striking example of non-Keatsian influence. Before 1848 he had not read the poet, and presumably he had not even read about him in the magazines or in such common works as the Boston reprints (1847, 1848) of Robert Chambers' *Cyclopaedia of English Literature* (Edinburgh, 1844). Hirst published the first canto of *Endymion. A Tale of Greece* in the *Southern Literary Messenger*, July, 1844.[36] In the *Weekly New Mirror*, July 27,[37] Willis described it as an imitation "after Keats." When he issued the entire poem, four cantos, at Boston in 1848, Hirst frankly confessed:

Before the publication of the first canto, I had never met with the Endymion of Keats, and purposely avoided the perusal of that beautiful poem until the completion of my own, with the express design of escaping the danger of unintentional plagiarism. This may appear singular; but it is easily explained. Until the age of twenty-three years, I entertained a holy horror of poetry—an almost ludicrous result of an exceedingly prosaic existence.

The *Albion*, June 3, 1848,[38] felt certain that Hirst's *Endymion* cannot "become very generally popular; for it is addressed to a class too small in number—to the class who delight in Keats and Shelley, and the highly imaginative school." Then, ignoring the attention given in its own columns to them, it went on:

How many have these two last named authors on their shelves, and how few are well acquainted with their contents! To relish them properly requires an abstraction from our routine of thought and occupation, which becomes more and more rare in the exciting times whereon we have fallen!

Dwight was much more favorably impressed with the contemporary *Endymion*. In the *Harbinger*, June 17, 1848,[39] he made an elaborate comparison of Keats and Hirst:

Hirst shows Endymion dreaming, and Keats dreams his dream. Both are legitimate forms of art; the first objective, and the latter more subjective. Hirst's is like sculpture; Keats' is like music. Hirst gives the story in a series of *tableaux vivants,* set in appropriate scenery; places Endymion before you in true Grecian marble; Keats renders into subtlest music all you feel and think and imagine as you gaze absorbed upon that statue. . . . [Keats] *is* Endymion. . . . He sits down to pour out his heart, to coin his life out into music. And of that life, the master spring and passion which inspires is love. Keats' "Endymion," amongst all the rhymed offerings which have been laid upon that altar, is preëminently *the* poem, the "Divine Commedia," we may say, of Love.

Hirst's poem lacks "the depth and warmth" of Keats, "the wondrous wealth of imagination," "the solemn classic grandeur, cheerful at the same time," of the glorious hymn to Pan, but "it is a genuine creation and of rare beauty." In Hirst, he concluded,

there are never any weaknesses, any stanza wrenched by duty from a listless mood, or any of the vagueness and the languor and the tremulous self-distrust and over-sensitiveness which punishes one-sided idealism, and which were the bane of Keats' most poetic life. . . . How affecting that too sincerely modest preface to his poem! The critics killed him. We do not fear this fate for the American Endymion.

Nor did *Holden's Dollar Magazine*, New York, July, 1848,[40] which admired Hirst's courage in writing "upon the same theme which Keats had almost made his own," but was scandalized to hear that he had not read Keats and that until the age of twenty-three he had "entertained a holy horror of poetry." Praising his "marvellous fluency of rhyme," his descriptions, and his "power of construction," it was, none the less, uncertain "whether it were better to be a well-paid lawyer, or an ill-paid poet." About this last point *Graham's Magazine*, July, 1848,[41] must have had no doubts, for it frankly preferred Hirst to Keats. The former's *Endymion*, it declared, is in tone

half way between Shelley and Keats, neither so ideal as the one nor so sensuous as the other. Keat's [*sic*] Endymion is so thick with fancies, and verbal daintinesses, and sweet sensations, that with all its wonderful affluence of beautiful things it lacks unity of impression. The mind of the poet is so possessed by his subject that, in an artistic sense, he becomes its victim, and wanders in metaphor, and revels in separate images, and gets entangled in a throng of thoughts, until, at the end, we have a sense of a beautiful confusion of "flowers of all hues, and weeds of glorious feature," and applaud the fertility at the expense of the force of his mind. . . . Art is not the prize of luck or the effect of chance, but of conscious combination of vital elements. Mr. Hirst, though he does [*sic*] give evidence of Keats' fluency of fancy and expression, has really produced a finer work of art. We think it is so important that a poem, to be altogether worthy of the name, should be deeply meditated and carefully finished, that we hazard this last opinion at the expense of being berated by all the undeveloped geniuses of the land, as having no true sense of the richness of Keats' mind, or the great capacity implied, rather than fully expressed, in his Endymion.

The Philadelphia *Endymion* answered another question. As A. J. H. Duganne[42] phrases it, "shall British critics . . . say *we* imitate? Who dares assert that Keats was read by Hirst?"

VI

GEORGE KEATS died at Louisville, December 24, 1841. He had long been unhappy because no life of his poet-brother was available to the public: his letters to Dilke harp upon his desire for any competent person—except Charles Brown—to write it. If George had been living in the middle forties, he would have been delighted when news reached America of the biography R. M. Milnes (afterwards Lord Houghton) was undertaking. But George was dead, his widow had re-married, and it was her husband, John Jeffrey, who hastened to offer his aid—and his new possessions. With considerable unction this man, whose unfaithful-ness and brutality were already making his wife com-pletely miserable, addressed Milnes on May 13, 1845, describing in general terms the Keats manuscripts of which he had "become possessed." In a subsequent letter of July 26[1] he gave a detailed list, and by September 8 he had finished making inaccurate transcripts, which he forwarded to Milnes.[2] His reward was a brief note of thanks, in which his name is not recorded, in the 1848 preface.

The faithful James Freeman Clarke, while visiting

Boston, Mass. Oct 31st 1845.

Dear Sir —

While on a journey through the Western States
this summer I heard that you were preparing a new
edition of the works of John Keats. Recently, on my
return to Boston, Mr Ticknor the publisher informed
me that there might perhaps be still time to communi-
cate with you before your book goes to press. I therefore
write in order to give you a copy of an autograph poem
of John Keats now in my possession, & hitherto unprinted in
any edition of his works. If you have not seen it, I think
you will be glad to have it. It was given to me some years
since by the poets' brother George, who resided in Louisville
Ky. where I also lived at that time. Geo. Keats was one
of the noblest & best of men, he possessed a piercing intellect,
a refined taste & pure intellectual culture. I account it the
greatest happiness to have known him. He had none of his
brothers' fancy, & his intellect though very keen was not I
think either so broad or so deep as that of John. But he
had the same woman's sensibility joined with the same
manly courage, for in my opinion John was thoroughly manly.
George loved & relished the old poets, & had an appreciating
love for his brother's poetry. He indeed revered him more than
he usually expressed, & his memory & fame was very precious
to him. It was always his favorite thought to return to
England & procure the publication of his brother's complete
poems under worthy auspices. I have heard him speak of
Dilk, the editor I think of the Examiner, as one to whom
he hoped to confide his brothers' MSS. When I heard that
you were to be the Editor I was happy in thinking how
much such an arrangement would have pleased George.

He died in 1841, a year after I left Kentucky, in the prime of manhood. He left a widow, since remarried to a Mr Jeffrey, & several children, two of whom, Georgiana & Emma, strongly resemble the portraits of John. George Keats had in his possession many unpublished poems of John, a part of a Drama, his letters (which were excellent & give you quite a new view of his intellect) & his copy of Spenser and of Milton, containing many pen marks & marginal notes. His notes written on the fly leaves of Milton, I printed in the Dial, edited by R. W. Emerson, No.   Two of his letters I also was allowed to print in the Western Messenger, some years ago. I trust you have been put in possession of all these papers by the family, but lest you should not have the lines to Apollo, I now transcribe them for you, just as they stand with the erasures & corrections. I hope that you will see the remarks on Milton in the Dial, some copies of which periodical found their way to England. I will not apologize for my freedom in thus addressing you, & will venture further to add that you are yourself well known & your poems loved by many in this country.

    Mr Geo. Keats had an excellent portrait of John, in water colors, well deserving to be engraved. It is a front face, looking up, with the chin resting on the hand. It was painted, I think, by Seaverns, John's companion in Italy.

                    with much respect
                    I am yours
                    James Freeman Clarke

R. M. Milnes, Esq —
        London

in "the Western States" during the summer of 1845, also read of Milnes' plans, and on October 31 he wrote, giving Milnes some general information about George Keats, John Jeffrey, and his own *Dial* (1843) article, and enclosing a partial transcript of the article and a complete copy of the ode "To Apollo." Clarke got no thanks at all. In a letter of December 12, 1872, he observes: "Lord Houghton did not acknowledge my letter; but he made use of the information contained in it, which was the essential point."[3] Later the two men carried on a sporadic correspondence, in which Samuel Osgood later joined, and mainly as a result of it Milnes at last (1876) categorically exonerated George Keats of meanness and cruelty to his brother. As an old man, Clarke wrote to Lord Houghton from Jamaica Plain, October 20, 1875, with unabated enthusiasm for his dead friend:

In thinking over what you told me of the charge made by some persons in England against George Keats, of having improperly used money of his brother—I am more than ever convinced that such a charge must be wholly unfounded. Of all men I have ever known he was the man least capable of such an act. He was not only a strictly honest man—but high minded & honorable in a high degree. All those who knew him while he lived in Ky. would say the same thing. More than this, his love & reverence for his brother John amounted to a sort of worship. All the three brothers, George, Tom, and John, seem, if we may judge by their letters, to have been very much attached to each other. It is far more likely that George should have advanced pecuniary aid to his brothers out of his own means, than that he should have ever made use of theirs. . . .

To the same correspondent on November 10, 1875, Clarke reiterated these convictions, saying that the charges against George were "simply incredible."[4]

John Howard Payne, too, made an effort to put Milnes in touch with American biographical sources. Writing from Paris on July 2, 1847, he told Milnes of the deaths of George and his daughter Isabel Keats, of the remarriage of George's widow, and, duplicating some of the material he had published in 1837,[5] of the letters and poems preserved in Louisville. Payne said that shortly he was returning to America, where he would gladly "execute any wishes of yours." Meantime, he enclosed a letter to G. D. Prentice, urging him to give Milnes every possible assistance; but the latter retained it in his files, no doubt because he had already heard from Jeffrey.

Milnes was pretty well known in America before George P. Putnam of New York published his *Life, Letters, and Literary Remains, of John Keats. . . . Complete in One Volume* (1848). Two volumes of his poems had been issued at Boston in 1846, and before that date his verses not infrequently were borrowed by the magazines,[6] in one of which he was characterized as "one of the best of the living poets of England."[7] Milnes himself (as well as his biographer, T. W. Reid) regarded the Keats book as comparatively unimportant. Thus he wrote to Varnhagen von Ense:[8]

I have published a Life and some remains of a remarkable young poet of the name of Keats, little known even in this country. It is the biography of a mere boy—he died at 24—, and therefore the literary interest is but small. . . . I cannot expect any reputation for the book, when the merits of the subject of it are so little known, but you and yours understand it better than we do ourselves, and thus may see something in it.

Milnes' poetry is now forgotten, his biography still mentioned with respect. "The reception of the book" in England, says Colvin,[9] "though not, of course, unmixed, was in all quarters respectful, and the old tone of flippant contempt hardly made itself heard at all." No such "flippant contempt" existed in America, and the book was well received.[10] The *American Literary Magazine,* Hartford, September, 1848,[11] paid Milnes a tacit compliment by printing a long essay on Keats. It declared:

The genius, the poetry, and the unhappy death of Keats are still and will ever be remembered. The sensitive plant, nipped by the rough blast of criticism, did not die without leaving behind at least its blossoms and "the promise of the fruit," which maturity would have ripened. Though his writings are imperfect and unfinished, still they will live. . . . The blow intended for the poem [*Endymion*] reached farther and struck the poet; and its injustice was acknowledged too late.

In much the same way the Philadelphia *Illustrated Monthly Courier*, November, 1848,[12] referred to assailants of Tennyson as "Keats-killers."

Among the more or less formal reviews, the *Literary World*, New York, September 9, 1848,[13] described the subject of Milnes' biography as "a poet, whose name is yearly growing into warmer repute and higher esteem, as that of one of the most gifted among the sons of song." It spoke of "the late, the almost reluctant, but full award of fame to Keats, as a man of rare genius," but did not agree with "the enthusiasts who would rank the performances of his half-developed powers with the matured productions of Byron, Coleridge, and Wordsworth." Had he lived "we might have had another Shakspeare in this creature of wondrous sensibility, to whom the Beautiful was alone an inspiration." In the opinion of the *Albion*, September 9,[14] "there has seldom issued from the press a volume of deeper interest, to those who can relish a high style of poetical composition, and to those who can mourn over genius laid low in early life." "This charming volume" has, to be sure, not exhausted the subject, for "there is an immensity of pith and marrow in Keats that will bear [further] examination and elucidation." A reviewer in the *United States Magazine, and Democratic Review*, October, 1848,[15] was more considerate of Milnes than of the latter's subject. He reminded readers that "Keats met with as much blind partiality and exaggerated applause from his immediate friends, as cold neglect from general readers, and bitter and unrelenting censure at the hands of those critics who swayed the popular taste." The "censure" was deserved, because the young poet had contempt for "the *Rules* of Art" until he wrote *Hyperion*. "In this and almost all his later poems, Keats reached a perfection of metre, a correctness and elegance of diction, not surpassed by the musical Byron himself." As for the poems Milnes includes: "Otho the Great is monstrous, and what is worse, undramatic. The fragment of the Cap and Bells . . . is too trifling is [*sc*. in] its details. . . . Of the minor poems and fragments the merit is fitful and occasional." "We have been induced to say more of the collection before us," he continued, "than its merits may warrant, by our deep sympathy for the sweet young poet, who wrote so much and so well; who . . . did not . . . leave a name 'written upon the waters.' His name is written in the hearts of all those who can love and appreciate a young and warm inspiration." He ended by expressing "a regret that Mr. Putnam . . . did not seize this opportunity of giving to the world the first *complete* edition of the works of Keats." *Graham's Magazine*[16] was somewhat patronizing: "From the time expended in its preparation, we expected a more satisfactory result." Indeed, Milnes gives little that is new, leaves many biographical facts dark. "Instead of proving that Keats was a strong man, he has very nearly proved that he himself is a sentimentalist." "The poems now published for the first

77471

time, though good enough to make a reputation, will hardly add to the fame of Keats."

Among other pronouncements on the biography perhaps those of C. A. Bristed,[17] Tuckerman, Lowell, and Amory D. Mayo deserve citation. In the *American [Whig] Review*, New York, December, 1848,[18] Bristed applauded Milnes highly: "Keats, *the poet*, we well knew, and had many pleasant memories of, from the time when our boyhood was first enlightened as to the wealth that was in him by the sweet criticism of Leigh Hunt." "Keats, *the man*, was a blank to us." Now Milnes has filled the blank. He has successfully demolished "the universal belief . . . that he [Keats] had died of the London Quarterly," showing instead that he "died of love." Bristed described Keats as "a genius without art, displaying marvellous beauties and glaring faults, gems and rubbish mingled," but insisted on "the steadily progressive improvement discernible throughout his productions." Tuckerman in the *Southern Literary Messenger*, December, 1848,[19] wrote that the biography of Keats "irresistibly attracts us to him as a man." "It is with the sensation of an intolerable pressure lifted from the heart, that we close the story." Lowell's opinion[20] was entirely favorable. In praising the excellence of Milnes' biography, he concluded:

Keats was a rare and great genius. He had, I think, the finest and richest fancy that has been seen since Shakespeare. And his imagination gave promise of an equal development. Ought we to sorrow for his early death, or to be glad that we have in his works an eternal dawn of poesy, as in Shakespeare we have early morning and full day? Forever and forever shall we be able to bathe our temples in the cool dew which hangs upon his verse.

Amory D. Mayo used Milnes as an excuse for an elaborate discussion of "The Poetry of Keats" in the *Massachusetts Quarterly Review*, Boston, September, 1849.[21] He believed, evidently with little reason, that Keats is "the English poet . . . with few exceptions the least known among us," but "he is an Artist of the first degree, embodying his conceptions, at times, in forms of surpassing beauty," "a great original poet," "the Spenser of modern poets," "in definiteness and beauty of form" superior to all modern English poets and barely below Chaucer and Spenser.

Since 1849 the opinions expressed by Lowell, rather than those by Mayo, have been generally shared by American critics and readers. Most would agree today that, as the *Southern Literary Messenger*[22] once phrased it, "The time for a criticism upon the *poetry* of Keats has gone by. His fame is secure. He drank the bright elixir and has become immortal. . . . He dwells amid the stars."

NOTES

NOTES

1. *The Life and Times of Tennyson* (New Haven, Conn., 1915), pp. 161 f., 316 f.

2. *John Keats: His Life and Poetry . . . and After-Fame* (London and New York, 1917).

3. "Keats and the Periodicals of His Time," *Modern Philology*, XXXII (1934), 37–53.

4. *Keats and the Victorians* (New Haven, Conn., 1944).

5. Page 541. Amy Lowell, *John Keats*, 2 vols. (Boston and New York, 1925), largely ignores the subject.

Notes to Section I

1. Edmund Blunden, *Keats's Publisher* (London, 1936), pp. 76, 83, 111 f.

2. I, 538.

3. For one, the *Poems* of 1817, given away by him, see p. 79, above.

4. Such quotations as this, for which no references are given, are taken from letters or other documents in the Harvard Keats collection.

5. *Notes and Queries,* August 6, October 1, 1932, CLXIII, 97, 249.

6. In "The Wild Sensitive," *Poems*, p. 62, she uses "leaf-fring'd stems," which Mabbott thinks borrowed from Keats' "leaf-fringed legend." The *Poems* has on its title-page the date "January, 1821." The poem preceding "The Wild Sensitive" is dated by Elizabeth's father January 1, 1819, the one following it January 1, 1820. Elizabeth seems to have been well read (several of her sonnets profess to be translations from Petrarch), but

the evidence for her acquaintance with "The Grecian Urn" is tenuous.

7. See p. 82, above.

8. Pages 225 f.

9. Van Wyck Brooks, *The World of Washington Irving* (New York, 1944), p. 245, says: "In much of his work he was influenced as largely by Keats as Halleck by Byron and Campbell."

10. F. L. Pleadwell, *The Life and Works of Joseph Rodman Drake* (Boston, 1935), pp. 13, 117.

11. J. G. Wilson, *The Life and Letters of Fitz-Greene Halleck* (New York, 1869), pp. 251 f., 264 f.

12. *Atlantic Monthly*, April, 1863, XI, 401. When E. C. Stedman (*Century Magazine*, February, 1884, XXVII, 603) visited Severn at Rome in 1879, the latter said he had brought Keats' poetry to the attention of Allston "and to that of seven or eight of his friends, though Allston was the only one among them who appreciated it."

13. II, 50 f.

14. LXXI, 434–437 (probably by G. F. Mathew).

15. VIII, 120–124 (mispaged 120, 117–120).

16. September, XIV, 245–248.

17. I, 372.

18. August 18, 1821, p. 527. It has "Bysshe."

19. I, 449–452, 460–465.

20. II, 315–321. See note 45, below.

21. Pages 1–26, prefixed to "Original Papers," volume I, 1821.

22. December 22, 29, 1821, I, 801–808, 819–825.

23. January, 1822, IV, 173–201.

24. X, 440 f.

25. Pages 40–43. For further references to Keats in other

issues of *Time's Telescope* see my notes in *Elizabethan Studies and Other Essays in Honor of George F. Reynolds* (Boulder, Colorado, 1945), pp. 294 f., and in the *Journal of English and Germanic Philology*, XLV (1946), 220.

26. April, 1821, III, 426 f. This article, which most Keats students have overlooked (parts of it are quoted in M. M.'s "On the Neglect of Genius," *Imperial Magazine*, London, December, 1821, III, 1077 f.), appears in the section called "Town Conversation. No. IV," and is signed "L." (the three earlier numbers are unsigned). Bertram Dobell, reprinting the article in *Sidelights on Charles Lamb* (London and New York, 1903), pp. 191–196, attributes it to Barry Cornwall. "L." was clearly a friend and admirer who had seen some of the letters in which Severn described Keats' last days. See pp. 18–20, above. The *London Magazine* in February, III, 210 f., had reviewed at length *Time's Telescope*, calling it "a very pleasant and useful little work." The latter then merely returned the compliment by borrowing, with a few changes, all the words quoted above from "Mr. Keats died" to "Italy," and from "Mr. Keats was" to "towards poetry."

27. XI, 487 (misprinted 478).

28. Blunden, *Keats's Publisher*, p. 129, reprints them in part from the *London Magazine*, June, 1822, V, 591.

29. Pages cxxv–cxxvii.

30. *A Sketch of Old England* (New York), II, 84–135.

31. Pages 169–171. The book was reviewed in Houston and Brooks' *Minerva*, New York, December 25, 1824, II, 186–188; in the *Atlantic Magazine*, New York, January, 1825, II, 203–215; and elsewhere.

32. II, 43.

33. The first two numbers (43 pages) are announced among "New Publications" by the *United States Review*, Boston and New York, September, 1827, II, 474.

34. 168 pages. "Printed by True and Greene. 1827."

35. It is praised in Mrs. Katharine A. Ware's Boston *Bower of Taste*, March 15, 1828, I, 173 f. She names Hill as the editor.

36. I, 23.

37. August, 1818, III, 519–524.

38. I, 136. The *Minerva*, of New York, however, published three of Shelley's poems in its issues for (cf. April 10, June 12) September 4, 1824 (I, 16, 160, 350), and January 8, March 5, July 30, 1825 (II, 223 f., 352, III, 272). Brief extracts from *Queen Mab* are given in George Bond's New York *American Athenaeum*, February 9, 1826, I, 440 (it also prints anonymously Keats' "Four seasons fill the measure of the year"), in which, on November 10, 1825, I, 293, C. W. P. had slurringly remarked, "We have had too many Voltaires, Rousseaus, Byrons, Shellys, and Godwins." References of one kind or another are made to Shelley in J. T. Buckingham's *New-England Galaxy*, July 6, 1827, and December 5, 1828. Willis paid him considerable attention in the *American Monthly Magazine*, notably in September, 1829, I, 431–436, where a long account of his poems, with quotations, is given; and in November, 1829, I, 554, where an "exquisite passage" from *Alastor* by "glorious Shelley" is quoted (it is reprinted in the *New-England Galaxy*, November 27). Julia Power, *Shelley in America* (Lincoln, Nebraska, 1940), has, unluckily, missed all these references, as well as important reprints by Kettell in the *New-England Galaxy*, mentioned below.

39. Or perhaps in New York, whence he wrote to Dilke on this date.

40. I, 161–163.

41. *Philadelphia Monthly Magazine*, July 15, II, 246 (see Julia Power, p. 71).

42. II, 329–332.

43. *New-York Literary Gazette*, April 29, 1826, II, 88 f.

44. Pages 135–150. Keats is treated on pp. 145–149; the others are Shelley, Michael Bruce, Charles Wolfe, and Herbert Knowles.

45. II, 315–321.

46. Compare the *London Magazine*, II, 315: "nothing more truly unprincipled than that abuse can be quoted."

47. So the *London Magazine*, II, 318, describes the ode as "distinct, noble, pathetic, and true."

48. Six other lines are quoted.

49. Fifteen lines are quoted from the opening.

50. Six other lines are quoted.

51. Compare the *London Magazine*, II, 320: "Cold-blooded conscious dishonesty . . . must have directed the pen of the critic . . . in the Quarterly Review."

52. II, 309–317. Four of these "Poetical Portraits," Bruce and Knowles being omitted, reappeared in the Providence, Rhode Island, *Literary Journal, and Weekly Register of Science and the Arts*, September 14, 1833, I, 114 f.

53. Page 186.

54. Who lived in Craigie House with Thomas Nuttall, curator of the Harvard Botanical Garden.

55. *New-England Galaxy*, p. 2.

56. As in the same, June 18, 1830, p. 2.

57. I, 360. This August number is reviewed in the *New-England Galaxy*, August 28, pp. 2 f.

58. August 22, 1829, VII, 50. Whether the four paragraphs he credits to "Boston Mercury" (see below) are all that Kettell printed cannot be told.

59. See pp. 7 f., above.

60. It is described as Volume XII, No. 621. Like all the others its four pages are not numbered.

61. Variants from the *Boston Mercury* (*M*), via the *New-*

York Mirror, and from the *London Magazine* (*L*) are given in footnotes.

62. So also in his reprint of the poem.

63. These two paragraphs replace these comments in *L:* We commence our article this month with but a melancholy subject—*the death of Mr. John Keats.*—It is, perhaps, an unfit topic to be discussed under this head, but we knew not where else to place it, and we could not reconcile ourselves to the idea of letting a poet's death pass by in the common obituary. He died on the 23rd of February, 1821, at Rome, whither he had gone for the benefit of his health. His complaint was a consumption, under which he had languished for some time, but his death was accelerated by a cold caught in his voyage to Italy.

64. There is but *L.* There is, unfortunately for his fame, but *M.*

65. *Omitted by L, M.*

66. the writings of this young man *L.*

67. yet they were full of high imagination and delicate fancy, and his images were beautiful and more entirely his own, perhaps, than those of any living writer whatever *L* (*M ends* than those of any author of his day whatever). *L and M go on:* He had a fine ear, a tender heart, and at times great force and originality of expression; and notwithstanding all this, he has been suffered [was allowed *M*] to rise and pass away almost without a notice.

68. *This sentence replaces in L and M:* the laurel, has been awarded (for the present) to [was awarded to *M*] other brows: the bolder aspirants have been [were *M*] allowed to take their station on the slippery steps of the temple of fame, while he has been nearly [he remained *M*] hidden among the crowd during his [his *omitted by M*] life.

69. and has at last died *L;* and died at last *M.*

70. and we must leave *L.*

71. many, however, even among the critics living, *L;* some, however, *M*.

72. observed by the Editor of the *L, M*.

73. no other Author whatever *L;* no other author *M*.

74. *L, M omit* as his.

75. love which *L, M*.

76. to bear towards *L, M*.

77. *For* return . . . nativity *L has:* return: that this has been too sadly realized the reader already knows.—

78. a brief *L*.

79. his *L, M*.

80. *Omitted by L, M*.

81. own *L*.

82. *M also substitutes the three sentences,* "Of these . . . to depart," *for* He was the youngest, but the first to leave us *L*.

83. is at last *L*.

84. Nine other lines are quoted here as in *L* and *M*.

85. *M ends here. L goes on:* There is something in this to us most painfully affecting; indeed the whole story of his later days is well calculated to make a deep impression. —It is to be hoped that his biography will be given to the world, and also whatever he may have left (whether in poetry or prose) behind him. The public is fond of patronizing poets: they are considered in the light of an almost helpless race: they are bright as stars, but like meteors
          "Short-lived and self-consuming."
     We do not claim the *patronage* of the public for Mr. Keats, but we hope that it will now cast aside every little and unworthy prejudice, and do justice to the high memory of a young but undoubted poet. L.

86. July, 1824, XL, 494–499. It includes the paragraph: "Keats died young; and yet his infelicity 'had years too

111

many.' A canker had blighted the tender bloom that overspread a face in which youth and genius strove with beauty.—the shaft was sped—venal, vulgar, venomous, that drove him from his country, with sickness and penury for companions, and followed him to his grave. And yet there are those who would trample on the faded flower—men to whom breaking hearts are a subject of merriment—who laugh loud over the silent urn of Genius, and play out their game of venality and infamy with the crumbling bones of their victim."

87. September, 1820, VII, 679, 681–684.

88. January, 1819, IV, 475–486.

89. *Edinburgh Review*, August, 1820, XXXIV, 203–213.

90. Kettell's changes are somewhat illuminating. Where in the second sentence Jeffrey spoke of "That imitation of . . . our older dramatists, to which we cannot help flattering ourselves that we have somewhat contributed, has . . .," he omitted the clause between commas. Jeffrey's "Keats, we understand, is still a very young man; and his whole works, indeed, bear evidence enough of the fact. They" is reduced to "Keats's whole works." "All the indulgence that can be claimed for a first attempt" is changed to "much indulgence"; "the earliest and by much the most considerable," to "the earliest." Whole sentences and sometimes parts of Jeffrey's quotations are omitted, as are his two paragraphs dealing with "Isabella" and the Nightingale Ode. It is worthy of note, however, that Jeffrey closes his review by quoting 44 lines from "Fancy," whereas Kettell gives the entire poem of 94 lines.

91. *American Monthly Magazine*, I, 723.

92. The same, August, 1830, II, 353–355. George Keats had a manuscript copy sent by Fanny Keats on May 31, 1826. See Rollins, *Publications of the Modern Language Association of America*, LIX (1944), 200 f.

93. Printed in the *New-England Galaxy*, August 27.

94. Just so he owned and edited the Boston *Amateur* from June 15 to November 22, 1830. The next issue, January 1, 1831, had a new owner and a new editor, W. J. Snelling.

Notes to Section II

1. Colvin, p. 527.

2. Edmund Blunden, *Shelley and Keats As they struck their Contemporaries* (London, 1925), p. 82.

3. The same, p. 83; see also Dorothy H. Bodurtha and W. B. Pope, *Life of John Keats by Charles Armitage Brown* (London, 1937), pp. 17–19.

4. William Sharp, *The Life and Letters of Joseph Severn* (London, 1892), pp. 165 f.

5. *Atlantic Monthly,* April, 1863, XI, 401. Even as late as 1892 J. G. Speed, George Keats' grandson, patriotically claimed (*Christian Union,* New York, August 20, XLVI, 332) that "lovers of Keats's poetry" are "more numerous perhaps in America than even in England."

6. See Keats' *Poetical Works,* ed. H. B. and M. B. Forman (New York, 1939), VI, cix f.

7. In the front of the first issue of the book is pasted a slip, announcing that portraits of the three writers will not be ready until January 15 next: "The volume being much demanded the publishers have thought it best not to await the completion of the engraving."

8. By Colvin, p. 527 n.

9. Pages 246–268.

10. See p. 38, above.

11. *New-England Galaxy,* XIII, 2. The contest was won by "Pedro," whose verse "Carrier's Address to the Patrons of the New-England Galaxy," January 1, 1831, Hill accepted and printed.

12. *American Monthly Magazine,* II, 639.

13. The same, June, 1831, III, 211 f.

14. They are listed in "New Publications," *North American Review*, July, 1831, XXXIII, 292, January, 1832, XXXIV, 276. The 1831 edition is reviewed, with reference to Coleridge only, in Sarah J. Hale's *Ladies' Magazine*, Boston, October, 1831, IV, 462–471.

15. E. P. Oberholtzer, *The Literary History of Philadelphia* (Philadelphia, 1906), p. 346.

16. *The Literature of the Middle Western Frontier* (New York, 1925), II, 24 f.

17. Three of these editions are listed in Rennell Rodd and H. N. Gay's *Bulletin and Review of the Keats-Shelley Memorial Rome* (London and New York, 1913), pp. 105, 157. S. F. Damon, *Amy Lowell* (Boston and New York, 1935), p. 691, also refers to three, asserting that "Keats had been recognized in America long before he was recognized in England." Colvin (p. 528 n.) mentions a separate edition of Keats' poems published at Buffalo, New York, in 1834, and he is echoed by Bodurtha and Pope, editing Charles Brown's *Life of John Keats*, p. 93. I know nothing of it, but Colvin got the idea from William Sharp's *The Life and Letters of Joseph Severn*, pp. 261 f., 264. There Sharp misinterprets a letter from Alfred Domett, who says that he bought a copy of the Coleridge-Shelley-Keats volume "so long ago as 1834 at 'Buffalo.' "

18. *Athenaeum*, August 1, p. 584.

19. Pages 356–368.

20. Page xiv.

21. *American Monthly Magazine*, March, 1831, II, 853 f. Willis quotes several of his pronouncements.

22. Samuel Parkman (class of 1834) gave the Porcellian Club, Harvard, a copy.

23. William Sharp, *The Life and Letters of Joseph Severn*, p. 170.

24. *Select Journal of Foreign Periodical Literature*, I, 36–46 (Critical Notices), following the *Westminster Review*, July, 1832, XVII, 34–52.

25. C. A. Bristed, writing on "American Poetry," *Fraser's Magazine*, July, 1850, XLII, 9–25 (see also his *Pieces of a Broken-Down Critic* [Baden-Baden, 1859], III, 25–30), remarks that in America "very copious editions of the standard English poets are sold every year, generally in a form adapted to the purses of the million; to further which end they are frequently bound two or three in a volume (Coleridge, Shelley, and Keats, for instance, is a favourite combination)," and that patriotic critics "take the line" that "*Evangeline* beats the *Eve of St. Agnes* 'all to smash.'"

26. Oddly enough O. A. Roorbach, *Bibliotheca Americana* (New York, 1849), pp. 155, 315, lists under Keats only Putnam's edition of Keats' *Poetical Works* and Milnes' biography. Under Coleridge (p. 63) he lists the Coleridge-"Shelly"-Keats volume by Crissy and Markley.

Notes to Section III

1. II, 575.

2. *New Age*, XXXVII (1929), 462.

3. H. E. Starr, in the *Dictionary of American Biography*, 1934, XIV, 593, finds "no record of his enrollment there."

4. Susan B. Riley, *The Life and Works of Albert Pike* (Nashville, 1934), p. 2, also gives these facts correctly.

5. See T. O. Mabbott, *Notes and Queries*, August 6, 1932, CLXIII, 97.

6. August, 1830, II, 298 f., 311–313; September, II, 376–378; October, II, 464–466; November, II, 523–525. Some are signed "A. P.," others are unsigned.

7. June, 1839, XLV, 819–830. Christopher North (p. 830), obviously unaware of any imitation of Keats, praises "these fine Hymns, which entitle their author to take his place in the highest order of his country's poets." In the "Autobiography" (p. 462) Pike calls the "Hymns" "the first thing I wrote worth anything." Later on, in the

"Literary Notices," probably written by the editor, Tuckerman, of the *Boston Miscellany and Lady's Monthly Magazine,* January, 1843, III, 43, we read: "Few American bards have manifested more of the true poetic fire" than Pike; "some of the imagery in his 'Hymns to the Gods' . . . is worthy of Keats."

8. *The Life and Works of Albert Pike,* p. 9.

9. December, 1829, I, 644–646; December, 1830, II, 603 f. The poem has his regular signature "A. P." Willis (the same, March, 1831, II, 859) says that Pike's " 'Hymns to the Gods,' published in this Magazine, and other things with the signature of his initial, speak for themselves."

10. II, 689. It is reprinted without credit but signed "Albert Pike" in the *Boston Pearl,* December 6, 1834, IV, 103 f. Pike is, I suppose, the P. who (*American Monthly Magazine,* July, 1830, II, 255), writing of the joys of cigar smoking, says, "to be with Shelley . . . with his lark, . . . to range the bottom of the sea with Keats, or sleep with him, with our eyes wide open, in the moon-light," or to read Coleridge, Byron, Scott, or Bulwer is "the most delicious thing in the world." Only a man "of good mind" can enjoy a cigar, "a man who relishes those nice little pleasures, which the *world* never enjoys—such a man as would like the beautiful little jewels of Keats, and the burning flashes of Shelley."

11. I, 240. Possibly he called it "Sonnet" because of the irregular length of the second poem.

12. November 15, 1834, IV, 83.

13. July, 1835, IX, 52. See also for references to Keats and Shelley his *Hymns,* pp. 252–257, and his *Lyrics and Love Songs,* p. 164, both edited by Lilian P. Roome (Little Rock, 1916).

14. *Prose Sketches and Poems,* pp. 134–136. In his preface Pike says: "I have not wilfully committed plagiarism. It is possible that the imitation may extend farther than I suppose. . . . The things of memory have become so confused with those of my own imagination, that I am

at times, when an idea flashes upon me, uncertain whether it be my own" or some other poet's.

15. E. E. Hale, *James Freeman Clarke* (Boston and New York, 1891), pp. 329 f.

16. Who in 1853 gave the Lowell Institute lectures on Shelley, Keats, and other poets. For his interest in Keats see further his *Ralph Waldo Emerson* (Boston and New York, 1884), pp. 92, 316 f., 405, and M. A. de W. Howe's *Memories of a Hostess* (Boston, 1922), pp. 43, 68, 206 f.

17. See E. W. Emerson, *The Early Years of the Saturday Club* (Boston and New York, 1918), pp. 282–286.

18. Professor Channing "took a special interest in him," according to T. B. Peck, *The Bellows Genealogy* (Keene, New Hampshire, 1898), p. 284.

19. But one member of the class of 1832, Henry Wheatland, founder of the Essex Institute, Salem, much later in life boasted that he had never read a line of Shakespeare or the other great poets. See *Henry Wheatland* (Salem, 1893?), p. 71.

20. *Life of Joseph Green Cogswell* (Cambridge, Massachusetts, 1874), p. 137.

21. The same, p. 350.

22. H. A. Beers, *Nathaniel Parker Willis* (Boston, 1885), p. 82.

23. See p. 23, above.

24. September, II, 417–419.

25. *John Lothrop Motley* (Boston, 1879), pp. 9, 11.

26. In the same, p. 14.

27. *Student Life* (New York, 1861), p. 37.

28. *Blackwood's Edinburgh Magazine*, September, 1824, XVI, 311.

29. *Old Cambridge* (New York, 1899), p. 14.

30. In Channing's *Lectures Read to the Seniors in Harvard College* (Boston, 1856), pp. xiii, xv.

31. *Student Life,* p. 109.

32. The same, p. 91.

33. *James Russell Lowell and His Friends* (Boston and New York, 1899), pp. 15, 22 f.

34. *Writings,* Riverside Ed. (Boston and New York, 1899), VI, 69 f.

35. E. E. Hale, *James Freeman Clarke,* pp. 96, 135.

36. The same, p. 107.

37. The same, p. 121, quotes only the first seventeen words.

38. In a letter of May 11, 1839, Henry Clay addressed Clarke, George Keats, Thomas H. Shreve, and others, who, "as a Committee" appointed "by a Club in Louisville . . . to procure the delivery of a series of Lectures in that City, with the view of introducing and encouraging a taste for intellectual and social pursuits and pleasures," had invited him "to deliver the first of the series on the second Monday of November next." He declined the invitation.

39. VII, 185–187.

40. This had been printed in the *Indicator,* June 28, 1820, p. 304, and the *London Magazine,* November, 1821, IV, 526.

41. Amy Lowell, *John Keats,* I, 113, observed that up to 1925 it had not been reprinted. It is in H. W. Garrod's *The Poetical Works of John Keats* (Oxford, 1939), pp. 539 f.

42. Payne's article is reprinted in the *Ladies' Pocket Magazine,* London, 1838, pp. 226–232. See Keats' *Poetical Works,* ed. H. B. and M. B. Forman (New York, 1939), IV, 37 f.

43. I, 763, 772–777, 820–823.

44. For the ode, see pp. 78, 95, above. For the letters (the second is given incompletely by Clarke) see M. B. Forman, *The Letters of John Keats* (London, 1935), pp. 154–157, 197–202.

45. Page 772.

46. (Cincinnati, 1891), pp. 74 f.

47. I, 180 f., II, 28 f. See also F. G. Peabody, *A New England Romance: The Story of Ephraim and Mary Jane Peabody* (Boston and New York, 1920), pp. 32–34, and C. L. F. Gohdes, *The Periodicals of American Transcendentalism* (Duke University Press, 1931), pp. 17–37.

48. Cist died in 1885, at which time (H. A. and Kate B. Ford, *History of Cincinnati* [1881], p. 265) he had "one of the finest collections of autographs in the world." It was sold in New York by the order of his executor, General Henry M. Cist, during 1886–1887, and the auction catalog runs to over 11,000 lots. Lot 2855 is a letter by Keats (No. 195, pp. 474 f., in M. B. Forman's 1935 edition of Keats' *Letters*), lot 2857 a letter by Mrs. George Keats, and lot 2856 apparently the letter of George I have quoted above. For Cist's biography and poems see W. T. Coggeshall, *The Poets and Poetry of the West* (Columbus, Ohio, 1860), pp. 337–342.

49. Venable, p. 79.

50. II, 28 f.

51. I, 259–264.

52. Leonora C. Scott, *The Life and Letters of Christopher Pearse Cranch* (Boston and New York, 1917), pp. 37 f.

53. Pages 43 f.

54. August, 1844, XXV (misnumbered XXVI), 94.

55. H. N. Gay, *The Protestant Burial-Ground in Rome* (London and New York, 1913), p. 5, remarks: "As early as 1816 the [Italian] guide-books had called the traveller's attention to the spot and the ciceroni had begun to traffic in its interest." There is a long description of it in Charlotte A. W. Eaton's *Rome in the Nineteenth Century* (Edinburgh, 1820), II, 172–175 (New York edition, 1827). William Berrian, assistant minister of Trinity Church, New York, in *Travels in France and Italy in 1817 and 1818* (New York, 1821), pp. 141 f., likewise

describes it ("a scene as secluded and peaceful as in the bosom of the country") and mentions the tomb "of a Mrs. Temple, who was born in Rhode-Island, and married an English baronet."

56. *A Journal of a Tour in Italy, in . . . 1821* (New York, 1824), p. 338.

57. W. H. Channing, *The Life of William Ellery Channing, D.D.* (Boston, 1880), p. 345.

58. J. W. Chadwick, *William Ellery Channing* (Boston and New York, 1903), p. 209.

59. IX, 449.

60. (London, 1835), I, 178, 202 f.

61. XL, 433 f. It is reprinted in *The Italian Sketch Book* (Philadelphia, 1835), pp. 56–58 (2d ed. [Boston, 1837], pp. 48–50). See also p. 65, above.

62. In *Graham's Magazine*, May, 1845, XXVI (misnumbered XXVII), 222, Tuckerman said: "The slab of Keats at Rome breathes a touching lesson to the young and susceptible aspirant for literary renown."

63. Susan Hale, *Life and Letters of Thomas Gold Appleton* (New York, 1885), pp. 199 f.

64. *Ward Family Papers* (Boston, 1900), p. 113.

65. Page 140.

66. In her notebook, a somewhat haphazard penciled affair, Miss Barker apparently dates her stay in Louisville as November 10–16, 1839. She mentions Clarke, "whom I saw every day & most agreeably—he is one of my *friends.*" Again she writes: "One of James Clarke's most valuable gifts was the acquaintance of Mr Keats the brother of the poet—to whom I am indebted for one of his original manuscripts." The notebook gives no account of her visit to the Protestant Cemetery, but it does have the undated entry, somewhere in Italy: "Gifford wrote the review that killed Keats—it is thought his being as it were the protégé of Leigh Hunt called it forth."

67. *Ward Family Papers*, p. 167; E. W. Emerson, *The Early Years of the Saturday Club*, pp. 109–116. From a granddaughter of Mrs. Ward the manuscript of the Autumn Ode passed to Amy Lowell and then into the Houghton Library.

68. *Letters from Italy* (New York, 1845), pp. 144 f. (Other editions appeared in 1846, 1848, 1853.) The whole passage is reprinted in the Boston *Pictorial National Library*, October, 1848, I, 179 f.

69. (New York, 1845), pp. 65 f.

70. *Views A-Foot* (New York, 1846), II, 326 f. The book reached its ninth edition by 1849, its twentieth by 1855. See also Taylor's *Life and Letters* (Boston, 1884), I, 130, for a reference (1848) to "Keats, whose spirit is now sitting at the other side of the table."

71. Pages 215–224.

72. Edward Cary, *George William Curtis* (Boston and New York, 1894), pp. 47 f.

73. *Early Letters*, ed. G. W. Cooke (New York, 1898), p. 264.

74. See p. 75, above.

75. *Life and Letters*, p. 343.

76. See pp. 86 f., above.

77. Pages 56 f.

78. *Six Months in Italy* (Boston, 1853), I, 428–430. The book reached a third edition in 1854. It may be worth adding that R. H. Dana and Mrs. Dana in 1881 thought the section of the cemetery in which Shelley lies a "spot where one would wish to lie forever." Dana was buried there on January 6, 1882. See C. F. Adams, *Richard Henry Dana* (Boston and New York, 1890), II, 388 f. Adams calls it "a spot than which none is more familiar to English-speaking visitors."

Notes to Section IV

1. (Philadelphia, 1936), pp. 3, 83.

2. *Pedlar's Progress* (Boston, 1937), p. 158.

3. V, 108.

4. XI, 154–174. See also Oberholtzer, *The Literary History of Philadelphia*, p. 266. Discussing Bryant, the *Southern Literary Journal*, Charleston, July, 1836 (II, 394), calls McHenry's "a shallow paper," and other magazines made less urbane comments.

5. Bryant knew *Hyperion* well enough in 1839 to say of Halleck's "Marco Bozzaris" (*New-Yorker*, January 11, VIII, 264), "We think, as we read it, of '—The large utterance of the early Gods.' " See also for references to Keats Bryant's *Life and Works*, ed. Parke Godwin (New York, 1883, 1884), II, 21, 316, V, 156.

6. Julius H. Ward, *The Life and Letters of James Gates Percival* (Boston, 1866), pp. 288 f. When Percival edited Vicesimus Knox's *Elegant Extracts* (Boston, 1842), he added (V, 375 f.) long extracts from *Endymion* and *Hyperion*.

7. *Fenimore Cooper* (New York, 1931), p. 138.

8. S. T. Williams, *The Life of Washington Irving* (New York, 1935), I, 193, says that Irving "hated the cockney group."

9. N. s., II, 89.

10. XIV, 119.

11. I, 409 f.

12. II, 332 n. (A review by Poe. See pp. 83 f., above.)

13. "Every body reads Campbell's poetry," said the *New-England Galaxy*, November 14, 1828, XI, 2.

14. XIX, 257.

15. XLIX, 81–96.

16. II, 106–121 (Critical Notices).

17. XXV, 535 (misprinted 435) f.

18. *The Life and Times of Tennyson,* pp. 383 f. Actually, as J. O. Eidson, *Tennyson in America* (Athens, Georgia, 1943), p. 6, shows, it was preceded by Clarke's review in the *Western Messenger,* December, 1836, II, 323–325, but it is the first comprehensive criticism.

19. In the *Christian Examiner,* Boston, January, 1838, XXIII, 305–327.

20. Page 306.

21. II, 97.

22. *Endymion,* I, 817 f.

23. V, 60, 589.

24. The same line is quoted in W. W. Story's address to the Harvard Musical Association, as printed in *Brother Jonathan,* New York, June 3, 1843, V, 123.

25. June 22, 1839, p. 167.

26. *The Literature of the Middle Western Frontier,* II, 23 f.

27. *The Flowering of New England* (New York, 1936), p. 183.

28. *Pedlar's Progress,* pp. 157 f.

29. *Bronson Alcott* (New York, 1940), p. 69.

30. *The Letters of Ralph Waldo Emerson* (New York, 1939), I, xxxvi f.

31. I, 149 f. But in his anthology *Parnassus* (Boston and New York, 1874) Keats is well represented (see pp. 34 f., 94, 128, 143, 509, 518).

32. Lowell refers to this remark in his 1885 lecture on Coleridge (*Writings,* VI, 69 f.): "I have heard this trinity of poets taxed with incongruity. As for me, I was grateful for such infinite riches in a little room, and never thought of looking a Pegasus in the mouth whose triple burden proved a stronger back than even that of the Templers' traditional steed."

33. *Mosses from an Old Manse* (Boston and New York, 1900), II, 185–188.

34. *American Literature,* II (1931), 430–432. Mabbott thinks that the essay was written by the journal's editors, E. A. Duyckinck and Cornelius Mathews.

35. III, 24–29.

36. III, 141.

37. May 10, 1820, p. 248.

38. III, 158. Incidentally, I have examined no newspapers in preparation for this sketch.

39. N. s., III, 403.

40. VIII, 37–41.

41. It is reprinted in his *Thoughts on the Poets* (New York and Boston, 1846), pp. 238–250 (3d ed., 1848; "New Edition," 1851).

42. In a letter of May 7, 1830, to Dilke, George Keats gives this same date. See pp. 11 f., above.

43. VI, 396; VII, 312; VIII, 569.

44. X, 241–246.

45. XX, 218–220.

46. *Rufus Wilmot Griswold* (Vanderbilt University Press, 1943), p. 9.

47. XXI, 152 f.

48. In Park Benjamin and James Aldrich's *New World,* New York, December 31, 1842, V, 409, an essay by Christopher North on "Our Young Poets" is reprinted. Of "the mob of gentlemen who write with ease," North wrote: "Shelley and Keats are their idols; and they, too, must needs sing of the Sensitive Plant and Ruth."

49. I, 3.

50. II, 152–154. It is included in his *Literary Studies* (New York, 1847). The quoted passages are on pp. 70, 73 f.

51. III, 37.

52. Reprinted in his *Lyric Poems* (Boston, 1854), pp. 5–7.

53. III, 495–504; reprinted in Clarke's *Memorial and Biographical Sketches* (Boston, 1878), pp. 221–229.

54. Clarke does not say that the "Remarks" are in Keats' hand. After Milnes had reprinted them (see p. 131, n. 3, below) and their authenticity had been challenged by Sir Charles W. Dilke (*Athenaeum,* October 26, November 2, 1872, pp. 529 f., 563), Clarke wrote (the same, January 4, 1873, p. 18): "These notes were not in the poet's autograph, but had evidently been transferred by his brother into his own copy of Milton, and very possibly he had not taken all of them." See Clarke's posthumous *Nineteenth Century Questions* (Boston and New York, 1897), p. 19, for a further comment on Keats and Shelley.

55. III, 331. Possibly some of her increasing enthusiasm for Shelley stemmed from the New York, 1845, edition (her autographed copy with notes by Emerson is in the Harvard Library) of G. G. Foster. The latter (p. 8) considered Shelley "the most perfect and entire [poet] in the language," "the prophet of a new era in the history of humanity."

56. I, 470–493.

57. The initials "M. M." are thus identified by G. W. Cooke, *Journal of Speculative Philosophy,* XIX (1885), 254.

58. R. W. Emerson and others, *Memoirs of Margaret Fuller Ossoli* (Boston and Philadelphia, 1852), II, 66.

59. See Madeleine B. Stern, *Publications of the Modern Language Association of America,* LVI (1941), 213.

60. The same, pp. 217 f.

61. *Papers on Literature and Art* (New York, 1846), pp. 58–99.

62. Caroline Ticknor, *Poe's Helen* (New York, 1916), p. 31.

63. I, 217–221.

64. I, 256.

65. Both Keats and Shelley fail to appear in C. D. Cleveland's *English Literature of the Nineteenth Century* (Philadelphia, 1853), a work "designed for colleges and advanced classes in schools, as well as for private reading."

66. Pages 193–210.

67. Pages 195 f.

68. E.g., pp. 154 f., 179, 182.

69. II, 17–20.

70. According to Bradford A. Booth, "Taste in the [American] Annuals," *American Literature*, XIV (1942), 299–302, Campbell was ignored by the compilers of annuals, while "Keats is virtually unknown, Coleridge and Shelley only slightly less so." Mr. Booth finds that Keats is represented by only five items as compared with 79 for Felicia Hemans, 65 for Maria Abdy, 47 for James Montgomery, 21 for Byron, 20 for Wordsworth, 13 for Coleridge, and 12 for Shelley. T. S. Arthur, editor of *The Brilliant; Gift Book for 1850* (New York), pp. 138–143 (see Ralph Thomson, *American Literary Annuals and Gift Books* [New York, 1936], pp. 35, 113), did include an essay on "The Poetry of Keats." According to him, "Keats, like Shelley, is oftener talked about than read; and there are hundreds who speak of him as a great poet, who cannot quote a line that he has written, nor mention an incident in his history." He gives extracts from four poems.

71. N. s., III, 411. On September 21, 1844, n. s., III, 449, the *Albion* reprinted from *Blackwood's*, September, 1844, LVI, 331–342, a review, in "North's old fashioned style of criticism," of Coventry Patmore, the last paragraph of which exclaims: "This is the life into which the slime of the Keateses and Shelleys of former times has fecundated."

72. *Anglo American*, New York, August 9, 1845, V, 372.

73. Joy Bayless, *Rufus Wilmot Griswold*, p. 88, says it really appeared in November, 1844.

74. In his sketch of Tennyson (p. 445) Griswold emphasizes the Keatsian influence.

75. *American [Whig] Review,* New York, July, 1845, II, 49–51; reprinted in Whipple's *Essays and Reviews,* 1850 (1851 ed., Boston, I, 350–354).

76. *North American Review,* October, 1845, LXI, 476.

77. Pages 490 f. Compare W. A. Jones, *United States Magazine, and Democratic Review,* New York, August, 1844, XV, 159: "Jeffrey has little of the poet in him. . . . He prefers Pope, we should suspect, to Pope's masters. Yet, strangely, in his later age, he conceived an unaccountable fondness for the poetry of Keats, a writer, one would think, quite out of the sphere of his literary sympathies."

78. *Early Letters,* ed. G. W. Cooke, pp. 190 f.

79. The same, p. 204.

80. See p. 53, above.

81. *Atlantic Monthly,* September, 1914, CXIV, 365; Caroline Ticknor, *Poe's Helen,* p. 23.

82. *Atlantic Monthly,* CXIV, 366.

83. *Poe's Helen,* p. 24.

84. *Atlantic Monthly,* CXIV, 371.

85. Leonora C. Scott, *The Life and Letters of Christopher Pearse Cranch,* p. 164.

86. Pages 230–255. Two extracts from the book, in each of which Keats is mentioned, are in the *Anglo American,* February 8, 1845, IV, 372, 373.

87. Page 248.

88. I, 417–431. The *Albion,* November 7, 1846, n. s., V, 533 f., reprinted from *Tait's Edinburgh Magazine,* October, 1846, XIII, 655–660, an article by Gilfillan on Hunt, in which he emphasized Hunt's and Keats' "barbarisms" of language. They "seem artificially twisted beyond the power of pronunciation in any human tongue, and fitted for the inhabitants of some other and still odder world than this."

89. 1845, pp. 103 f. The best discussion of this passage is in C. L. Finney's *The Evolution of Keats's Poetry* (Cambridge, Massachusetts, 1936), I, 90 f., 275 f.

90. XVIII, 71.

91. II, 75 f.

92. II, 234.

93. II, 360.

94. So, too, *Graham's Magazine,* August, 1846, XXIX, 106, said: "Spenser and Keats seem to have inspired the poet, as well as Shakspeare."

95. XXX, 83.

96. XIII, 81–84.

97. LXIV, 467.

98. XXX, 117.

99. As on pp. 30, 32 f., 163.

100. (1851 ed.), I, 475, 477, 482, 484.

101. XXXI, 107 f.

102. XXI, 427–429. Another essayist, December, p. 511, speaks of "the feminine delicacy of Keats."

103. XXXI, 42.

104. See his *Poems* (London, 1850), p. 98, and *Howitt's Journal,* London, December 11, 1847, II, 382.

105. N. s., VII, 76 f. The *Daguerreotype,* Boston, February 5, 1848, II, 24–29, and *Littell's Living Age,* Boston, March 4, 1848, XVI, 446–450, reprinted from *Tait's Edinburgh Magazine,* December, 1847, XIV, 850–854, Gilfillan's article on "Mrs. Shelley," which refers to Keats as "the purest specimen of the ideal—a ball of beautiful foam, 'cut off from the water,' and not adopted by the air."

106. Page 241 (probably from Lester's *Criticisms* [London, 1847], which I have not seen).

107. *North American Review,* April, 1848, LXVI, 459 f.

Notes to Section V

1. February 21, pp. 149 f.

2. "Her poetry has the essence of immortality," said the *New-York Literary Gazette,* May 6, 1826, II, 105.

3. *The Origins of American Critical Thought,* p. 3.

4. Brainard's *Literary Remains,* 1832, pp. 21 f.

5. II, 151–157.

6. *Holden's Dollar Magazine,* June, I, 323.

7. Poe's *Poems,* ed. Killis Campbell (Boston, 1917), pp. xliv, 1, 169 f., 212.

8. *Southern Literary Messenger,* January, III, 49. See a mention of Keats in Poe's *Works,* ed. Stedman and Woodberry (Chicago, 1895), VI, 256.

9. *Works,* VI, 121. See p. 122, n. 12, above.

10. The same (1894), I, 60.

11. G. E. Woodberry, *Century Magazine,* January, 1903, LXV, 447.

12. *Thomas Holley Chivers* (New York, 1930), p. 90.

13. Keats was not known to the editors and contributors of *The Orion, A Monthly Magazine of Literature, Science, and Art,* three volumes, published at Penfield, Georgia, during 1842–1843, and, judging from B. H. Flanders' *Early Georgia Magazines* (Athens, Georgia, 1944), to the other periodicals published in that state.

14. Printed in *The Lost Pleiad; and Other Poems* (New York, 1845), p. 23.

15. *Letters* (New York, 1894), I, 138 f.

16. XX, 199. Again, C. J. P., in the *Ladies' National Magazine,* Philadelphia, March, 1844, V, 97, found in "The Legend of Brittany" in his *Poems,* 1844, "many things . . . that remind us of Keats. Like all of his productions it has, often, an exuberance of fancy approaching to effeminacy."

17. Pages 10, 73.

18. Pages 101 f.

19. Page 103.

20. XXVI (misnumbered XXVII), 142.

21. See also Lowell's *Literary Essays* (Boston and New York, 1890), I, 218–246 ("Keats," 1854) and 289 ("Of all English poets, Keats was the one to have translated Homer").

22. Pages 137–139. Keats does not appear in *The Waif: A Collection of Poems* (Boston, 1845), probably because Longfellow chose its contents "Not from the bards sublime," but from "some humbler poet." For later references to Keats see Longfellow's *Life* by Samuel Longfellow (Boston and New York, 1891), III, 220, 289, 401. His sonnet "Keats" was written in 1873.

23. Pages 122–124.

24. Pages 159 f.

25. XI, 499.

26. XIII, 300.

27. IV, 108.

28. *Uncollected Poetry and Prose*, ed. Emory Holloway (New York, 1932), I, 133.

29. *The Complete Prose Works of Walt Whitman* (New York, 1902), VI, 120. See the same, III, 289, IV, 23, VI, 84, 128. Striking later comments are in Horace Traubel's *With Walt Whitman in Camden* (New York, 1908, 1914), II, 518, III, 83.

30. So his novelist brother, John Esten Cooke, informed Griswold on June 6, 1851. See W. McC. Griswold, *Passages from the Correspondence . . . of Rufus W. Griswold* (Cambridge, Massachusetts, 1898), p. 196. Later on another Southern poet, Lanier, owned a copy of a Philadelphia edition which Federal soldiers pillaged from him: see A. H. Starke, *Sidney Lanier* (Chapel Hill, North Carolina, 1933), p. 57.

31. XXX, 324.

32. *Broadway Journal*, New York, May 24, 1845, pp. 328–331.

33. July, 1845, XXVII (misnumbered XXVIII), 47.

34. *Poems*, pp. 82–95.

35. Pages 17–31.

36. X, 440–444.

37. See also "Ephemera" in his *Miscellaneous Works* (New York, 1847), p. 134.

38. N. s., VII, 273.

39. VII, 55.

40. II, 438.

41. XXXIII, 57.

42. *Parnassus in Pillory. A Satire* (New York, 1851), p. 44.

Notes to Section VI

1. It is mentioned by H. W. Garrod, *The Poetical Works of John Keats*, pp. xxxviii, l.

2. They are now in the Harvard Keats Collection. With justice J. G. Speed, *The Letters of John Keats* (New York, 1883), p. ix, remarks: "Mr. Jeffrey evidently exercised his own discretion in making selections from the letters, and just as evidently did not exercise a very wise discretion." According to E. F. Madden (*Harper's New Monthly Magazine*, August, 1877, LV, 358), Milnes borrowed from Speed's mother, Emma Keats Speed, presumably after 1848, Severn's water-color sketch of Keats and various manuscripts. Mrs. Speed and Sarah F. Clarke (Madden, pp. 359 f.) also supplied in 1875 part of the funds necessary for the repair of Keats' grave and monument.

3. For the letter see the *Athenaeum*, January 4, 1873, pp. 18 f. Milnes (see p. 125, above) printed the Milton anno-

tations and the Apollo ode at I, 274–281, II, 255 f., with no acknowledgments. Probably Clarke also sent him the copy for Keats' journal letter to Tom, July, 1818 (No. 75 in M. B. Forman's 1935 *Letters*, pp. 170–175), that is printed at I, 160–166. The original, endorsed "Copied August 1845," is still among Clarke's papers at Harvard.

4. He is replying to a letter Lord Houghton wrote from Philadelphia on November 6: "Would you dislike to write a couple of pages respecting the position and character of George Keats in Louisville—which I will insert in the book [the Aldine edition, 1876]? Your personal observation will give an authenticity to the story which my bare assertion will not do."

5. See p. 44, above.

6. Greeley's *New-Yorker*, VIII, 243, IX, 40, 131, published one of his poems on January 4, 1840, three on April 4, and one on May 16.

7. The same, July 25, 1840, IX, 301. He is, however, treated rather cavalierly in Thomas Powell's *The Living Authors of England* (New York and Philadelphia, 1849, pp. 196–202). But Powell, an English expatriate, confesses, "we do not belong to the inner and devoted circle of his admirers."

8. Walther Fischer, *Die Briefe Richard Monckton Milnes'* . . . *an Varnhagen von Ense* (Heidelberg, 1922), p. 122.

9. Pages 537 f.

10. Much later Thomas Bailey Aldrich, whose signature with the date of July 29, 1865, appears on a flyleaf in the Harvard copy, wrote at the head of the dedication in his copy, "To natural dullness Milnes adds a carefully acquired bad prose-style."

11. III, 168–178. The *Eclectic Magazine*, New York, July, 1848, XIV, 409–415, reprinted from *Hogg's Weekly Instructor*, Edinburgh, 1848, n. s., I, 145–148, a very eulogistic critical and biographical sketch of Keats that was written before Milnes' life appeared.

12. I, 78 f. According to Eidson, *Tennyson in America,* p. 65, the writer was Hirst.

13. III, 621–623.

14. N. s., VII, 441 (misprinted 144).

15. XXIII, 375–377. *Littell's Living Age,* October 7, 1848, XIX, 20–24, reprinted from the *Spectator,* August 19, XXI, 803–805, a review of Milnes.

16. November, 1848, XXXIII, 297 f.

17. In *Five Years in an English University* (3d ed., New York, 1874) Bristed discusses the "Apostles" and the Sterling Club and their effect on current literary judgments. On one occasion (p. 320) he called on a fellow student who was about to take the Classical Tripos examination. "*Some* allusion to the examination it was not possible to forego, but we soon disposed of the shop with our tea, and then read, criticized, and very generally talked over the poets of the new school—Shelley, Keats, Tennyson, Miss Barrett—for some hours."

18. VIII, 603–610.

19. XIV, 711–715.

20. *Letters* (1894), I, 138 f.

21. II, 414–428. The article is anonymous, but see Gohdes, *The Periodicals of American Transcendentalism,* p. 168.

22. In another review of Milnes, October, 1852, XVIII, 598–601.

INDEX

INDEX OF NAMES AND TITLES

*(John Keats is not indexed but his poems are included
among titles)*

144

THIS FIRST EDITION CONSISTS OF
SEVEN HUNDRED AND FIFTY COPIES
Printed by
D. B. UPDIKE THE MERRYMOUNT PRESS
BOSTON